Laura Ingalls Wilder

A Family
Collection

Laura Ingalls Wilder

A FAMILY
COLLECTION

Life on the Farm and in the Country

Making a Home

The Ways of the World

A Woman's Role

Edited by RICHARD MARSHALL
With illustrations by SUSAN STERNAU

BARNES
&NOBLE
BOOKS
NEW YORK

Acknowledgments
Grateful acknowledgment is made for the invaluable help provided during the compilation of this book by the Library of the Missouri State Historical Society in Columbia, Missouri, and by the Huntington Memorial Library of Oneonta, New York; with special thanks to Huntington librarians Carolyn Lathey, Thomas Rushmer, and Sarita Smith.

This edition published by Barnes & Noble, Inc.

1993 Barnes & Noble Books

Book design by Charles Ziga, Ziga Design

ISBN 1-56619-051-7

Printed and bound in the United States of America

M 9 8 7 6 5 4 3 2 1

Contents

The Ways of the World

A Woman's Role

Introduction

Laura Ingalls Wilder was sixty-five years old when her first book, *Little House in the Big Woods*, was published in 1932. By the time the last volume in the story of her life as a pioneer girl, *Those Happy Golden Years*, was published, she was seventy-six and world famous. Her books had been translated into forty languages, including German and Japanese editions published at the request of General Douglas MacArthur at the end of World War II. MacArthur believed that the Little House books would have a wholesome influence on the children of America's former enemies, and he was probably right: children in faraway places found Laura's stories of pioneer life in America as exotic as tales of Egypt, Amazonia, and the Himalayas might have been for Laura's young American readers. ("The children wouldn't let me stop writing," she once said, wonderingly.) For older readers, too, Laura's books had, and still have, a wonderful, intimate strangeness. How did this modest "farm woman" (as she called herself in her early journalism) win the loyalty of such a large and diverse audience?

Laura belonged to the last generation of America's true pioneers, and because of it she saw the world from a unique perspective. She had lived in log cabins and in a sod-house. She had heard Indian war drums. She had seen the days of the prairie schooner pass to those of the train, the automobile and the airplane. By the time she wrote the Little House books, she had lived through two World Wars, and had seen American society change beyond recognition. She wrote of a world long passed, but she wrote for a period and for readers she knew well. She knew what would seem as strange as a lunar landscape to children of modern cities and the modern countryside. She knew what values would resonate for her adult readers like the chimes of some distant golden age. She knew her readers, she knew her stories, and long before she even began to write the Little House books, Laura knew how to tell what was in her heart. And, as the articles collected here show, she served a long apprenticeship in print. When Laura sat down to write the incomparable stories of her life, she was well prepared.

THE STORIES OF A LIFE

In the Little House books Laura records, with vivid and cheerful realism, the wonder of growing up in a brand new land. She tells of danger, hardship, and self-reliance made strong by adversity; she tells of family closeness. In her first book, *Little House in the Big Woods* (1932), she wrote about how she grew up in Minnesota's dense forests with Ma, Pa, and Mary. In her second book, *Farmer Boy* (1933), she described her husband Almanzo's childhood near Malone, New York. And then her books told how the course of her life and Almanzo's gradually converged.

Her most famous book, *Little House on the Prairie* (1935), describes how Pa, longing for the space and isolation of the frontier, took his family to Indian Territory in Kansas. Here Laura saw Indians for the first time, wanted a "papoose" of her own, and heard war drums beating in the night. When the government forced settlers to move out of the Territory, the family went north again and settled near Walnut Grove in Minnesota.

On the Banks of Plum Creek (1937) describes the family's life in a sod-house set in the bank of a creek near Walnut Grove. It tells how Laura went to school, got wonderful Christmas presents, saw a plague of locusts descend on the land, and watched her father set out to walk 200 miles to find work (at $1 a day) in eastern Minnesota. It was during the Walnut Grove period that Laura's sister Mary became blind, and Laura began to "see out loud" for her (as she describes in Chapter 3 of *By the Shores of Silver Lake*). At this early age, then, Laura began to translate the colors of the world into words.

When Pa found work on the new railroad that was being built across the prairie, the family moved to South Dakota. The story is told in *By the Shores of Silver Lake* (1939). The town of De Smet grew up beside the railroad tracks, and the Ingalls built yet another home on the claim they'd staked just outside town. In *The Long Winter* (1940), Laura tells how the small town would have starved during the dreadful winter of 1880-81, but for the heroism of Almanzo and of Cap Garland. *Little Town on the Prairie* (1941) describes the life of the town and Laura's schooling and early teenage years. In *Those Happy Golden Years* (1943) she tells the story of her first job as a teacher, and of her courtship by Almanzo; and in *The first Four Years* (written in the late 1940s, but not published until 1971), Laura tells how she and Almanzo married, struggled for a livelihood on their homestead, and had their first child, Rose; she tells how their second child died within days of his birth, and how Almanzo was crippled by diphtheria; and, finally, how their house and almost everything they owned was lost in a fire.

And there the Little House books end, with Laura only twenty-two, and her daughter Rose still an infant. Laura's diary of the wagon journey with Almanzo and Rose to their final home in the Missouri Ozarks appeared in 1962 as *On the Way Home*, and a collection of letters written to Almanzo from San Francisco in 1915 was published in 1974 under the title *West from Home*. But apart from these glimpses, the years of Laura's life from 1889 to 1932 have been lost to us. What else happened to the Wilders? How did things work out in Missouri? Everyone who has read the Little House books knows the feeling: at the end of the saga, we want more. We know these people as if they were our own family, and we don't want to say goodbye to them in drought-stricken De Smet. We don't want to leave them at the door of their little bare shack on the new land in Missouri. We want to know what happened next.

The Years of the *Ruralist*

Now we do know what happened next, and we know it in Laura's own words. For in 1911 she began to write articles for the Missouri *Ruralist*, a widely read farm paper. Here she first gained the confidence and skill that allowed her, much later, to write the Little House books, and here she explored for the first time some of the themes that later delighted her millions of readers. The articles, poems, stories, reminiscences, wry comments, and philosophizings on the ways of the world that are collected here were written between 1911 and 1918, and they made Laura one of Missouri's best-read commentators—"a writer and state leader," as the *Ruralist's* editor, John Francis Case, said. They also fill the gap in our knowledge of Laura Ingalls Wilder. Here at last, in her own words, is what became of the twenty-two-year-old Laura we left in De Smet, South Dakota. What kind of woman was she?

By the time Laura wrote her first article for the *Ruralist* she was forty years old. It was called "Favors the Small Farm Home," and it spoke of the very particular and pioneering sense of community that marks all of Laura's books (most of all, perhaps, *Little Town on the Prairie*). It was published because Laura had gained a great reputation in the Ozarks as a poultry breeder, and had become a popular speaker at farmers' meetings. On one occasion she was too busy to give her speech in person, so she sent a copy of it to be read for her. John Case, the editor of the *Ruralist*, was in the audience that day, and he liked what he heard. He got in touch with Laura, and asked her to send him some articles for his paper. "Favors the Small Farm Home" was published on February 18, 1911. It occupied almost a full page, was given a prominent headline, and carried a small but flattering picture of Laura. Beneath it was presented the dissenting opinion of one of America's great agronomists, Professor Liberty Hyde Bailey, director of the Agricultural Research Station at Cornell University, New York, who wanted to see people return to village life rather than to small farmsteads.

Laura's first article was followed the next month by a poem billed as "one of Mrs. Wilder's Nature Songs." It was called "The People in God's Out-of-Doors," and is Laura's first published celebration of the love of nature that distinguishes the Little House books.

By 1916, Laura was writing regularly for the *Ruralist*, and in July, 1917, she was appointed editor of the paper's home section. Her success was due—in her editor's opinion—to the fact that "She knows farm folks and their problems as few women who write know them." And Laura's articles do indeed deal with a great variety of problems, ranging from rural loneliness to the best way to feed hens in winter and how to organize a social club. She often illustrates her points with stories about people she knows, behavior she observes, or events in her own life (many of which she later retold in the Little House books). She discusses stories in the news (she speaks passionately of the Great War, for example), and she frequently deals with social issues, most strikingly with the movement for women's rights. She also provides her readers with lively accounts of such national events as the great San Francisco Exposition of 1915, and tells the stories of women whose lives she feels will inspire her readers. Her articles often run counter to accepted opinion. She thinks that women should beware of becoming obsessed with housework, because there are better things in life. She favors labor-saving devices, and can hardly wait for kitchens to be sensibly designed (though she thinks this probably won't happen till a woman does it). She thinks that getting a suntan, far from being unladylike, is a badge of honor for those who work out of doors. She insists that the only real partnership between a man and woman is one of perfect equality, and she firmly supports the movement for women's rights.

LAURA'S FAMILY

Sometimes Laura's views provoked critical and even angry replies from her readers. Some of those replies have been reprinted here alongside the articles that inspired them. A few of the readers' recipes that Laura thought prizeworthy have also been reprinted and, occasionally, a *Ruralist* news item is used to illuminate the context of one of Laura's topics. She considered the farm families that she wrote for to be, in a modern term, her extended family (and so it seems especially proper that some of her readers, including children, should have their own voice here), and she had much sound advice to give them about family and social virtues.

Laura spent the first twenty-two years of her life as a pioneer child, girl and wife, and the pioneer virtues she learned—those of hard work, self-help, and caring for and helping others—were the bedrock of her life.

She learned endurance and optimism, many times over, from Pa. She learned economy from Ma, patience from her sister Mary, and from strangers like Mr. Edwards, nicknamed "the Tennessee wildcat," she learned the virtue of neighborly kindness (she tells in *Little House on the Prairie* how he walked miles through the night and waded across a river to bring Christmas gifts for her and Mary). From her future husband Almanzo Wilder she learned courage when he risked his life to bring food to the starving town of De Smet.

These were the ideals she passed on to her readers, at first in her *Ruralist* articles and later in her books. Of course, she passed on more purely personal things, too. She shared her humor with her *Ruralist* readers, occasionally writing in a wry way about the love of her life, Almanzo, the "Man of the Place." She wrote of fashion, and what a farm woman might make of current trends. She spoke, often, of her delight in nature, and of her sense that all God's creature's, including birds and animals, shared a certain equality, and were all, in the most inclusive sense, part of one family.

A NOTE ON THE TEXT

The articles collected here were originally written by Laura Ingalls Wilder for the Missouri *Ruralist* between 1911 and 1918. They are clues, in her own words, to the years most of us thought were missing from the story of Laura's life. They tell us how she lived, what she thought about, and where her affections lay. They are her prelude to the Little House books, and they allow us, for the first time, to glimpse the stages by which America's greatest children's writer mastered her craft.

The articles have been arranged by theme, and within thematic groupings are in chronological order. The original spelling and punctuation have been preserved, and each article is presented in full. Brief introductions have been added to some pieces, and there are explanatory notes at the end of each section.

Life on the Farm and in the Country

The People in God's Out-of-Doors

I love to listen to the bird songs every day
And hear the free winds whisper in their play,
Among the tall old trees and sweet wild flowers.
I love to watch the little brook
That gushes from its cool and rocky bed
Deep in the earth. The sky is blue o'er head
And sunbeams dance upon its tiny rivulete.
I love the timid things
That gather round the little watercourse.
To listen to the frogs with voices hoarse,
And see the squirrels leap and bound at play.
Then, too, I love to hear
The loud clear whistle of the pretty quail,
To see the chipmunk flirt his saucy tail,
Then peep from out his home within the tree.
I love to watch the busy bees,
To see the rabbit scurry in the brush,
Or sit when falls the dewy evening's hush
And listen to the sad-voiced whippoorwill.

—From Mrs. Wilder's Nature Songs

My Apple Orchard

*Written for Missouri **Ruralist** by A. J. Wilder,*
Rock Ridge Farm, Mansfield, MO

How a "Tenderfoot" Knowing Nothing About Orcharding Learned the Business in Missouri—Quail as Insect Destroyers

Although this article (and the one following) is credited to A. J. Wilder—Almanzo—Laura probably helped with the writing, and may even have written the whole thing herself. (Almanzo wasn't fond of talking about himself, and when Laura wrote *Farmer Boy* she had to drag the stories out of him). In any case, "My Apple Orchard" is an interesting account of how Laura and Almanzo shared the work at Rocky Ridge Farm (not "Rock Ridge Farm," as the subtitle has it). Each of them knew every single tree in their orchard, and, as the story of the quail shows, they were unusually sensitive to the value of preserving the natural balance of the environment.

When I bought my farm in the fall, some years ago,[1] there were 800 apple trees growing on it in nursery rows. Two hundred had been set out the spring before, in an old wornout field, where the land was so poor it would not raise a stalk of corn over 4 feet high. This field was all the land cleared on the place; the rest of the farm was covered with oak timber.

I have always thought it must have been a good agent who persuaded the man of the place to mortgage it for 1,000 apple trees when the ground was not even cleared on which to set them. However he unloaded his blunder onto me and I knew nothing about an orchard; did not even know one apple from another. I did know though that apple trees, or indeed trees of any kind could not be expected to thrive in land too poor to raise corn-fodder, so whenever I made a trip to town I brought back a load of wood ashes from the mill and a load of manure from the livery barn and put it around those trees that were already set out in the field.

I cleared enough land that winter on which to set out trees from the nursery broke it the next spring and put in the trees after I had worked it as smooth as I could. The trees already set out were 25 feet apart in the rows and 32 feet between the rows so I set the others the same way. I dug the holes for the trees large and deep, making the dirt fine in the bottom and mixing some wood ashes with it.

The trees I handled very carefully, not to injure the roots and spread the roots out as nearly as possible in a natural manner, when setting the trees. Fine dirt was put over the roots at first and pressed down firmly, then dirt was shoveled in to fill the hole. Some more wood ashes was mixed with the dirt when it was being shoveled in. I did not hill the dirt up around the tree, but left a little cupping for conserving moisture. All trash was raked away, leaving it clean and smooth, and again I used some wood ashes, scattering them around the tree, but being careful that none touched it to injure the bark. The ashes were used altogether with the idea of fertilizing the soil and with no idea of any other benefit, but I think they may have saved my orchard.

It is confessing to a colossal ignorance, but I found out later that I had planted woolly aphis on nearly every one of my apple tree roots. At the time I thought that for some reason they were a little moldy. I read afterward in an orchard paper that lye from the wood ashes would destroy the woolly aphis and save the tree and as the use of wood ashes was kept up for several years I give them the credit for saving my trees.

As I never allowed hunting on the farm, the quail were thick in the orchard and used to wallow and dust themselves like chickens in the fine dirt close to the tree. I wish this fact to be particularly noted in connection with the other fact that I had no borers in my trees for years.

A near neighbor set out 2,000 trees about the same time and lost seven eights of them because of borers. He used every possible means to rid his trees of them except the simple one of letting the quail and other birds live in his orchard. Instead he allowed his boys to kill every bird they saw.

My apples were sound and smooth, not wormy, which I also credit to the birds for catching insects of all kinds, as I never sprayed the trees. Within the last few years the hunters, both boys and men, have been so active that it has been impossible to save my quail and so I have had to begin the eternal round of spraying, and cutting the trees to get the borers out.

When I set the trees I trimmed them back a good deal. While I knew nothing of the science of trimming I knew that I did not want a forked tree, so I trimmed to one stem with a few little branches left at the top. I watched the trees as they grew and trimmed away while they were very small all the branches that would interlock or rub against another branch.

In the fall I always whitewashed the trees to keep the rabbits from gnawing the bark and if the storms washed it off I whitewashed them again. Every spring they were whitewashed in April as a sort of house-cleaning and to make the bark smooth, so it would not harbor insects, for I found that if there was a rough place there was where the eggs of insects were deposited.

Between the trees I raised corn, potatoes and gardened until the trees were 8 years old, when I seeded the land down to timothy and clover. Of course when I raised crops I fertilized them enough to make them grow and the trees always got their share. As a result I get a good hay crop out of the orchard making two good crops from the land. I think that one thing that has made my orchard a success is that I took individual care of each tree. What that particular tree needed, it got. Wife and I were so well acquainted with the trees that if I wished to mention one to her I would say "that tree with the large branch to the south," or "the tree that leans to the north," etc. The tree that leaned was gently taught to stand straight so that the sun would not burn the bark. This was done by tying it to a stake, firmly driven into the ground on the south side of the tree and from time to time shortening the string which held it.

The trees came into bearing at 7 years old and the apples were extra well colored and smooth skinned. I have had apple buyers[2] and nursery men tell me that my orchard was the prettiest they ever saw, and my Ben Davis are different than any I have ever seen in being better colored and flavored and in the texture of the flesh. People even refuse to believe that they are Ben Davis,[3] at times. My orchard is mostly Ben Davis and the rest is Missouri Pippin.[4] If I were to start another orchard I would plow and cultivate the land for several seasons to prepare it for the trees. The wildness and roughness should be worked out in order to give the little trees a fair chance. Then I should plant apple seed where I wanted the trees to stand, and then bud, onto the sprout, the variety I wished to raise. In this way the tap root would not be disturbed as it is by moving the tree, but would run straight down. This makes a longer-lived, stronger tree.

Did You Ever Can Cider?

There's a woman in Iowa, according to the Country Gentleman, who cans many gallons of cider each year, and it tastes mighty good in the winter with cookies and doughnuts or in fruit cake and mincemeat. To can cider fill clean jars with it, fit on the rubbers and tops, and submerge them in a hot water bath for sterilization, boiling 20 minutes.

—Stella Gertrude Nash

The Story of Rocky Ridge Farm

*Written for the Missouri **Ruralist** by A. J. Wilder,[5]*
Wright County, Missouri

How Mother Nature In the Ozarks Rewarded Well Directed Efforts After a Fruitless Struggle On the Plains of the Dakotas. The Blessings of Living Water and a Gentle Climate

Ruralist Editor's Note:—Among the stories received in the course of our farm home story contest,[6] the following came from Mr. Wilder, with the request that it be published, if worthy, but that it not be considered an entrant for any prize. We certainly consider it worthy—one of the most helpful and interesting—and believe all contributors to this feature will approve of our giving it good position on this page since we cannot give it a prize.[7]

To appreciate fully the reason why we named our place Rocky Ridge Farm, it should have been seen at the time of the christening. To begin with it was not bottom land nor by any stretch of the imagination could it have been called second bottom. It was, and is, uncompromisingly ridge land, on the very tip top of the ridge at that, within a very few miles of the highest point in the Ozarks. And rocky—it certainly was rocky when it was named, although strangers coming to the place now, say "but why do you call it Rocky Ridge?"

The place looked unpromising enough when we first saw it, not only one but several ridges rolling in every direction and covered with rocks and brush and timber. Perhaps it looked worse to me because I had just left the prairies of South Dakota where the land is easily farmed. I had been ordered south because those prairies had robbed me of my health and I was glad to leave them because they had also robbed me of nearly everything I owned, by continual crop failures. Still coming from such a smooth country the place looked so rough to me that I hesitated to buy it. But wife had taken a violent fancy to this particular piece of land, saying if she could not have it she did not want any because it could be made into such a pretty place. It needed the eye of faith, however, to see that in time it could be made very beautiful.

So we bought Rocky Ridge Farm and went to work. We had to put a mortgage on it of $200, and had very little except our bare hands with which to pay it off, improve the farm and make our living while we did it. It speaks well for the farm, rough and rocky as it was that my wife and myself with my broken health were able to do all this.

A flock of hens—by the way, there is no better place in the country for raising poultry than right here—a flock of hens and the wood we cleared from the land bought our groceries and clothing. The timber on the place also made the rails to fence it and furnished the materials for a large log barn.

At the time I bought it there were on the place four acres cleared and a small log house with a fire place and no windows. These were practically all the improvements and there was not grass enough growing on the whole forty acres to keep a cow. The four acres cleared had been set out to apple trees and enough trees to set twenty acres more were in nursery rows near the house. The land on which to set them was not even cleared of the timber. Luckily I had bought the place before any serious damage had been done to the fine timber around the building site, although the start had been made to cut it down.

It was hard work and sometimes short rations at the first, but gradually the difficulties were overcome. Land was cleared and prepared, by heroic effort, in time to set out all the apple trees and in a few years the orchard came into bearing. Fields were cleared and brought into a good state of fertility. The timber around the buildings was thinned out enough so that grass would grow between the trees, and each tree would grow in good shape, which has made a beautiful park of the grounds. The rocks have been picked up and grass seed sown so that the pastures and meadows are in fine condition and support quite a little herd of cows, for grass grows remarkably well on "Rocky Ridge" when the timber is cleared away to give it a chance. This good grass and clear spring water make it an ideal dairy farm.

Sixty acres more have been bought and paid for, which added to the original forty makes a farm of one hundred acres. There is no waste land on the farm except a wood lot which we have decided to leave permanently for the timber.

Perhaps we have not made so much money as farmers in a more level country, but neither have we been obliged to spend so much for expenses and as the net profit is what counts at the end of the year, I am not afraid to compare the results for a term of years with farms of the same size in a more level country.

Our little Rock Ridge Farm has supplied everything necessary for a good living and given us good interest on all the money invested every year since the first two. No year has it fallen below ten per cent and one extra good year it paid 100 per cent. Besides this it has doubled in value, and $3,000 more, since it was bought.

We are not by any means through with making improvements on Rocky Ridge Farm. There are on the place five springs of running water which never fail even in the dryest season. Some of these springs are so situated that by building a dam below them, a lake of three acres, twenty feet deep in places will be made near the house. Another small lake can be made in the same way in the duck pasture and these are planned for the near future. But the first thing on the improvement program is building a cement tank as a reservoir around a spring which is higher than the buildings. Water from this tank will be piped down and supply water in the house and barn and in the poultry yards.

When I look around the farm now and see the smooth, green, rolling meadows and pastures, the good fields of corn and wheat and oats; when I see the orchard and strawberry field like huge boquets in the spring or full of fruit later in the season; when I see the grape vines hanging full of lucious grapes, I can hardly bring back to my mind the rough, rocky, brushy, ugly place that we first called Rocky Ridge Farm. The name given it then serves to remind us of the battles we have fought and won and gives a touch of sentiment and an added value to the place.

In conclusion I am going to quote from a little gift book which my wife sent out to a few friends last Christmas:

> Just come and visit Rocky Ridge,
> Please grant us our request,
> We'll give you all a jolly time—
> Welcome the coming; speed the parting guest.

Economy in Egg Production

Laura was famous for getting her hens to lay in winter, "when no one else could," and her skill as a poultry-raiser helped the Wilders survive the early, difficult days at Rocky Ridge Farm. Here she shares her expertise with her readers. Egg production was an important part of a small farm's economy, and (as Laura points out in "All in the Days Work"), it was usually a woman's responsibility, for which she rarely got much credit. In "Doing Our Best," she pays tribute to the young members—mostly female—of the *Ruralist* Poultry Club, and, as she often does in her articles, puts a humdrum activity into a broad social and moral context.

To economize in the feeding of our hens, we should try to get results with as little expenditure of time and acreage as possible. We cannot produce eggs more cheaply by feeding less. It works rather the other way, for it takes a certain amount of food to keep up the body of a hen and that naturally comes first with her. Whatever food of the right kind that she eats, over and above what is necessary for the upkeep of the body, goes to the making of eggs. If the wrong kind of food is given, the surplus goes to fat and unless we wish to market the hens this extra feed is wasted.

Some corn is necessary in winter to keep up the bodily heat, but a little corn thrown to the hens is not enough for them to manufacture eggs from, nor is it better feeding to throw them a little more corn. Corn is a heating, fattening food and feeding of corn alone, or of too much corn, simply makes the hens fat and does not produce eggs.

Corn is also more expensive than some other feeds that are better for our purpose. The same ground with the same amount of work will produce much more feed if planted to milo.[8] Milo is said to have produced 40 bushels of seed on ground that would not raise 10 bushels of corn and the seed contains 80 per cent of the feeding value of corn. Jerusalem corn, kafir,[9] and cowpeas,[10] are also fine for hens and will grow more feed to the acre than corn.

Cowpeas especially are good. The hens will eat both the peas and the leaves and while feeding on them the hens will lay remarkably well. It is fine to have some planted near enough so that the hens can pasture on them and harvest whatever peas get ripe.

Some stock beets should be raised to feed the layers in winter. The hens are fond of them and they act as a relish and appetizer as well as save other feed.

Sunflowers can be raised in odd places. They will grow very good heads without cultivation and for this reason can be grown in fence corners and other places where nothing else can be raised to advantage. The seeds are very rich and will make the plumage of the fowls bright as well as increase the number of eggs, and all they cost is the planting of the seed and the gathering of the heads.

Now, with the right crops planted to furnish our grain feed, let us see what can be done with the waste of the farm. Small vegetables, cabbages that have failed to head well and some turnips should be saved at gathering time to feed the hens in winter, when they will not be able to get green food. They like vegetables and the parings from vegetables either raw or cooked.

Let the hens help the hogs save the skimmilk. Meat scraps are rather expensive to buy and skimmilk will take their place to a certain extent. Meat in some form is necessary if the hens are to lay well so if possible give them what skimmilk they will drink.

When the butchering is done there are a good many scraps and waste pieces that should be fed to the hens. Not all at once, as too much at a time will make them sick, but a few each day until they are used up. The lights, kidneys and livers should be cut up in small pieces before feeding. The scraps from pressing out the lard are also good. These will all help save the grain feed, besides being just what the hens need.

Another good plan is to save the wheat and oats in the bundle for feeding the hens. It saves the thresh bill and is much better for the hens to let them do their own threshing.

One very important thing in producing eggs cheaply is to produce the eggs. Otherwise what we do feed is wasted. To get the eggs we must feed a variety and if a part of this is what would be saved in no other way, we are turning this waste material into cash.

And Missouri "Showed" Them

FROM A TO Z—ALFALFA TO ZINC—
THE "SHOW ME STATE" WON HONORS AT 'FRISCO'S EXPOSITION

This article, packed with detail and colorful observations, ran with a banner head-line in the *Ruralist,* and was a breakthrough in Laura's writing career. It was based on visits she made to the International Exposition in San Francisco during her stay there with her daughter Rose in September and October of 1915. See also a sec-ond article in this section, in which Laura dwells lovingly on the Fair's food exhibits. Laura wrote to Almanzo almost every day while she was away from Mansfield, and her letters, full of wonder and excitement, have been published under the title *West from Home.* In them she describes how she is still "learning to write," and how Rose (who was by then an established journalist) is helping her to "block out" some of her articles, though not all of them, and perhaps not this one: in a letter written to Almanzo on October 22, she says that she has "mapped out for myself the work for the *Ruralist.*"

*M*issouri has taken more prizes at the International Exposition than any other state in the Union except California, and Missouri's mines have beaten, on its own ground, the Golden State of the Forty-niners. Missouri has met all the states of the Union, all the countries of the world, in fair competition, and has made a proud record.

In agriculture alone Missouri has won the Grand Medal of Honor, 17 gold medals, 21 silver medals, 15 bronze medals, besides two honorable mentions, which go to Henry county. In education the state has carried off the silver medal.

Missouri's mines won the Medal of Honor, 6 gold medals, 54 silver medals, and one bronze medal. Our livestock exhibitors received cash prizes amount-ing to $6,834 and eight ribbons. In processed fruit Missouri won the silver medal. Awards in horticulture were still to be made when this was written.

In hospitality, too, Missouri has been a charming example to many sister states. Our beautiful Colonial Home, on a grassy avenue overlooking the Avenue of the States and the blue waters of San Francisco Bay, has won the reputation of being the most homelike and inviting at the great fair.

The portico with its pillars, and the broad flights of steps leading up to it, gives an impression both dignified and hospitable. From it, one steps through wide glass doors into a spacious reception hall, finished in white enamel and furnished in dull blue velvet. This great room, more than 80 feet long, with a high beamed ceiling, combines with its feeling of space an effect of cosiness and comfort, given by a huge fireplace, soft-toned velvet rugs and big inviting armchairs.

Large French doors of glass open from it on to a rear plaza, which fronts directly on the sparkling blue Bay, dotted with the white sails of innumerable tiny yachts. From this plaza, sheltered from the ocean winds by the wings of the building, one sees, across the expanse of water, the mountain ranges of Marin county, Tamalpais, Muir woods, and dozens of little towns. The view is inspiring and beautiful.

A feature of the building which has been a revelation to thousands of visitors is the library in one of the wings. Its shelves contain more than 1,500 volumes, all written by Missouri authors. Hundreds of persons have been surprised to learn here for the first time the fact that our state has produced more successful authors than any other in the Union.

On the lower floor of the building, besides the rooms already mentioned, are the rest-rooms, a large board-room and offices for the commission. At the second floor level a balcony overhangs the reception hall, and opening from it are the bedrooms for the members of the commission and their families. The advantages of architectural arrangement, as well as its beauty, have been widely praised, and it is a credit to the artistic skill of the Missourian who designed it, Senator H.H. Hohenschild of Rolla. Within a few weeks of its completion, by the McCarthy construction company of Farmington, dozens of local and national societies had requested to be allowed to hold meetings or give social affairs there. Hon. D.S. Smith, vice-chairman of the commission, who has been in charge of all Missouri's activities at the fair, found time somehow in his crowded days to uphold the reputation of our state for hospitality.

The popularity of the building grew, and every week since the fair began it has been the scene of at least one brilliant social or philanthropic gathering. Mrs. D.S. Smith has been a charming hostess at these affairs, acting with the official hostess, Mrs. James B. Gantt, of Jefferson City, and their popularity with the best people of the Pacific Coast has reflected no little credit upon Missouri's social ability.

Our showing in horticulture is very good indeed. In this department Missouri processed fruits have already taken the silver medal, and the whole exhibit is very attractive. No Missourian, I am sure, has gone through the Palace of Horticulture without feeling justifiable pride in that array of apples, nuts, watermelons and flowers, beautifully displayed under green-latticed archways. I noticed especially the apples, which were not surpassed in size, coloring, or flavor by any shown at the fair.

It is a pity that the ruling of the Exposition directors has prevented all states east of the Rockies from entering into competition for the awards on apples. These awards will be made only on five boxes of orchard-packed fruit, and the shipping distance makes it impossible for any but near-by states to get them to the fair in good condition. However, the people at the fair do not see the prizes, they see the fruit, and not a state in the Union has sent better fruit to the fair than Missouri.

Their keeping qualities, too, are proved by the fact that a great many of the apples on the tables were shown last fall at the Sedalia State Fair.

I was glad to see, also, that our watermelons were the best in the entire building, not even excepting the Burbank displays, or the exhibit of the Turlock district, which is California's great melon-growing region. Scarcely anyone who passed through our exhibit while I was there failed to notice and comment on this.

While our native-grown black walnut is perhaps not quite so aristocratic as the California English walnut, still no nut that grows equals it in richness and flavor. In our state nature bountifully supplies this delicious nut, with no trouble or expense to us, while the Californians must plant, graft, cultivate, irrigate and spray their English variety. The jars of walnuts, hickory nuts, and hazel nuts displayed in our horticultural exhibit were for this reason a striking illustration of Missouri's natural advantages.

The whole display was very ably handled by Director Charles W. Steinman, of Dalton, and his assistant, John McDemott of Montgomery county, and the horticulturists of Missouri can feel that they have done the state full justice.

Nearly 20,000 Missourians had already registered at our agricultural booth, under the great tower with its electric sign, "Missouri," which is conspicuous from any part of the Palace of Agriculture, when this was written in November. This tower, 65 feet in height, stands in one corner of the space allotted to our state, and is the principal feature of the display. It is literally covered with Missouri corn, from the arches up to the top, an impressive spectacle which is given added point by a sign stating, "Missouri produces one-tenth of the world's corn." The archways themselves, through which one passes in going under the tower, are decorated with excellent specimens of oats, wheat, kafir, maize, timothy, alfalfa, tobacco and cotton, arranged attractively on a background of dull blue cloth.

It was distinctly a pleasure to me to observe how excellently well these products compare with those grown in other states. Indeed, with the exception of the alfalfa, which of course competed with that grown under irrigation in the intensely hot California interior valleys, I saw no specimens exhibited anywhere, and even in alfalfa Missouri won a bronze medal awarded to Scott county.

When I came through the archways under the tower and stood in the main exhibit space, I fairly jumped with surprise. There on the wall was a picture of Governor Major, more than life-size and more than life-like, made entirely of corn. I would have recognized it anywhere for Missouri's governor, and almost anywhere for Missouri corn, so the artist who designed and worked it out may feel he has done full justice to both his subjects. Above the governor's pictured head an American eagle, made of corn husks, oats and kafir, stood proudly out on the blue cloth background, while above the eagle the state seal was displayed, also made of grains.

Other Missouri products were shown in glass cases, arranged in the main floor space. Except the tower with its decorations, and a skillful use of cotton, grain and grasses in trimming the rest of the exhibit, no attempt was made to produce a spectacular effect. Missouri went to the fair to show, in a business-like way, what she could do in agriculture at home, and she did it. She is bringing home the Grand Medal of Honor.

We surprised our fellow exhibitors in the livestock section, but it was a surprise that re-acted upon the Missouri commission itself. The commission, to encourage our local livestock breeders, had offered to double the amounts won by them at the Exposition. Now the members of the commission are all enthusiastic boosters for Missouri. They expected to make a good showing in livestock; indeed, they expected to make a very good showing. But, sanguine as their expectations were, they had not supposed they would be called upon to double $3,200 in prizes, as they had to do when the Exposition awards were announced. Goodness knows what would have happened to the pocketbook of the commission if the whole of our livestock had reached the fair. Five hundred thousand dollars worth of Missouri cattle, gathered, inspected, and ready to ship West from Kansas City, was refused by the Exposition directors, on account of a ruling quarantining the Exposition against all cattle from the Middle West. There is no doubt that if that exhibit had gone through we would have had a much larger share of the livestock prizes, but as it was our breeders won enough to startle the commission, and to flatten its purse considerably.

Our jennets carried off every prize offered in their class. Sixteen little beauties, exhibited by Monsees & Son, won $1,790 in prizes. It is interesting to note that the jennet who carried off all honors at the St. Louis Exposition was beaten here only by her daughter, who is now champion.

Our saddle horses—beauties, every one of them, with their slim dainty legs, heads held high, and bright, intelligent eyes—were one of the most popular exhibits in the livestock section, and they won substantial proof of their fine qualities, $1,410 in cash prizes, and a number of ribbons.

EDUCATIONAL EXHIBITS WERE FINE

The increased interest in educational methods, and systems of child-training, which has grown so rapidly in the last few years, made the Palace of Education one of the most popular buildings at the grounds. Here were shown school work, educational methods, and handicraft of children from New York state to the Philippines, China and Japan. Madame Montessori herself came from Italy to take charge of a class of tiny children in this building. Entered thus in competition with the whole world, Missouri won the silver medal. I must admit that this was a surprise to me. We are so likely to see the defects in institutions close at hand and imagine that farther away conditions are so much better.

When I realized the place Missouri takes in education I felt greater interest in our school problems, and while there are still many improvements possible, I am sure we should all be very much pleased, and proud of this award.

Our commissioner of education, Norman Vaughan, and his assistant, W.N. Laidlaw deserve great credit for the demonstration they have given of Missouri's school system. Our decentralized method is shown by a system of tiny electric lights, representing children, which flash on and off, showing the pupil's progress from grade to grade and from school to school, without any unnecessary loss of time.

A mammoth map of the state, also dotted with electric lights, shows our high school growth from 1894 to the present day. At a glance, while the groups of lights flash on and off, one literally sees the high schools multiply, and multiply again. The sight shows quickly, and in a very impressive manner, the really extraordinary growth in the number of our high schools.

Views of the Missouri University, the five state normal schools, and other colleges and high schools, are shown on an illuminated screen, the pictures changing automatically every 20 seconds. The whole exhibit has attracted the interested attention of educators from all over the world, and it is a pleasure to wander about it and listen to their comments.

When Otto Ruhl of Joplin took charge of our mining exhibit at the fair he intended to show Missouri mines to the best possible advantage. Without intending it he has also shown another Missouri characteristic of which we should be as proud as we are of any product of our state. He has given an exhibition of thrift. With only $6,500 to spend, he arranged a display which is more attractive to the eye, more instructive and interesting, than Nevada was able to show with $27,000. He also has won for us a Medal of Honor, seven gold medals, 54 silver medals, and one bronze, standing second only to Nevada among all the states, and leaving California, with her great mining industries, far behind.

Beginning with the mine itself, every process in handling the ore is shown, from the raw quartz in the ground to the finished product. The idea is good, and the way it is carried out is perfect. The display occupies 3,000 feet of floor space, in a long strip down one side of the Palace of Mines and Metallurgy. It is surrounded by a low wall, built up to give the exact appearance of a mine— all the ores showing among the native rock and flint exactly as they are found in our hills. Above this wall great columns covered with zinc and lead concentrates, support cornices of zinc metal. Thus from first sight of the place, the eye follows the progress of the metal from the mines to the finished product.

The entrances are three great arches, one of zinc, one of lead, and one of our Carthage marble. Inside, one sees first a model Joplin mine, showing in detail the tunnels, the little cars and railways used underground, the exact rock formation of the mine, and the buildings on the surface. Following this are the crushers, and a concentrating plant, which show the method of bringing our low-grade 2 per cent ore, ready for smelting. After this, one comes to the finished product, shown in wash boards and fruit jar covers.

Beside these cases, displaying the zinc as it enters our kitchens, were cases containing specimens of lead and zinc ores, which were beautiful enough to hold the attention of everyone who saw them. Several specimens of lead ore here contain 68 per cent of pure lead, an impossible proportion according to all the books, for theoretically, a 67 per cent lead ore is the highest possible. However, here are the actual specimens, with 68 per cent. What does Missouri care for theories, when she beats them in actual facts? On the outside of these blocks of almost pure lead, are iron pyrites and pure lead crystals.

Missouri's Crystal Springs, too, are represented here by a beautiful display of mineral waters, shining through dozens of bottles, and accompanied by pictures of the springs.

Another unique exhibit to our credit are the clays, which no other state had shown. Here, too, the whole process from the raw earth dug from the St. Louis quarries, to its final appearance in roofing tiles, sewer pipe, garden ornaments and statuary. It might have taxed almost any brain to devise an attractive display of sewer pipe and roofing tile, but Mr. Ruhl has solved the difficulty. He built up the sewer pipe into a tall flagpole, and designed the American flag from the roofing tile, in red, white and blue.

Beside the clays are the coal, supplied by Macon, Randolph, and Barton counties, and the iron, which comes from Crawford county. Specimens of Missouri granite appear here also, the red granite being perfect in texture and coloring. Nor are these the only products of Missouri's mines. Hannibal has represented her cement industry by samples showing every step of its production from shale and limestone to cement blocks, brick and tile.

AMAZING AND UNEXPECTED THINGS

Huge slabs of tripoli, that stone of so many amazing uses, have been the center of a great deal of attention. It is a fine, smooth rock, looking with its colored veinings, something like a cake of Castile soap, and I was amazed to find it the parent of dozens of familiar things, Sapolio, Gold Dust, Bon Ami, Old Dutch Cleanser, and practically all other scouring soaps, are made from it.

Another display was startling to me. I have been a Missourian for nearly 30 years, but I had to travel to the Exposition to find out that there is in my state a mining industry entirely controlled by farmers. A mining industry, moreover, which brings in an income of $250,000 to $300,000 a year. This tremendous sum goes to the farmers of Washington county, in payment for their mining of barytes.

The depth of their mines is little more than the depth of a plow-furrow. Barytes, a valuable stone, the use of which has made possible our fine magazine pictures, is found on Washington county farms, on or near the surface. In the fall the farmers plow and dig out the rock, pile it up until the rains have washed it clean of clay and gravel, and then haul it to town, like so much cord wood.

All in the Day's Work

Just a Neighborly Visit With Folks at Rocky Ridge Farm

Laura was keenly aware that the work of America's farm women was generally unacknowledged and underappreciated, and here she introduces a theme that she explores in detail in her articles on the role of women in American life. She also touches here upon the feelings of loneliness, monotony, and even madness that many farm women suffered. Laura had seen all these at first-hand when she left home to work as teacher and lodged with the Brewster family. In chapter 7 of *Those Happy Golden Years,* "A Knife in the Dark," she describes how she witnessed a horrifying moment in the life of a woman made frantic by isolation and poverty. No doubt this experience—she was only fifteen at the time—helped to shape Laura's understanding of the problems of rural loneliness, and perhaps contributed to a fear of insanity. In *On the Way Home,* her diary of the wagon journey from De Smet to Mansfield, she describes the "awful" sight of an "idiot," a "full grown man," near Bridgewater, South Dakota, and later tells how though Almanzo wanted to stop and visit the asylum at Yankton, she "could not bear to."

One hundred and seventeen thousand dollars was paid for poultry, eggs and cream, in the town of Mansfield during 1915. Of this amount $58,000 was paid for eggs alone, $39,000 for poultry and $28,000 for cream.

During the time of the turkey drives $10,000 in ten days was paid for these farm products by the produce men of Mansfield.

A big turkey drive is quite a sight to see. There were several came to Mansfield just before the holidays. In one drive alone there were 650 turkeys. Six hundred and fifty Christmas dinners for somebody walked into town in a drove.

I wonder if Missouri farm women realize the value in dollars and cents of the work they do from day to day in raising farm products for the market? How many persons when reading the astonishing amount received in a year for Missouri poultry and eggs think of the fact that it is practically all produced by the women, and as a sideline at that! For of course a woman's real work is the keeping of the house and caring for the family. Not only the care of the poultry, but the raising of garden products and small fruits is largely women's work; and in many instances the greater part of the labor of producing cream and butter. The fact is that while there has been a good deal of discussion for and against women in business, farm women have always been business women, and I have never heard a protest.

A friend of mine has a large tree in her back yard that she calls her turkey tree. Out of this tree every fall she gathers $100 worth of turkeys. If one could only have unlimited numbers of trees like that! But, unfortunately, there are a great many like another friend of mine who lost all the chicks she hatched last summer. The rats took them, sometimes a whole flock in a night. I raised 300 chicks myself by keeping the coops as far away from the buildings as possible. But every morning I wondered whether I should find them alive or stacked up in a pile somewhere.

When one thinks of the difficulties under which poultry and eggs are brought to the market, the wonder is that the amount is one-tenth as great. There are all the diseases to which chicks are heir to be contended with and besides there is a hawk in every treetop and a rat in every corner waiting for them as soon as they come out of the shell. I feel sure if Governor Major had ever tried to raise chickens on a farm he would not have vetoed that bill placing a bounty on hawks. And why not a bounty on rats? They are a perfect nuisance around the buildings and frightfully expensive to feed, besides the loss of the young chicks they kill. And I'm sure no one could say a word in their favor.

Learning how to rat-proof buildings does not help much with the old buildings. We keep a continual war on rats with traps and poison and cats. Once in a while we get the place well cleared, but soon they swarm in again. If everyone would take care of their own rats it would simplify matters. But they do not and so the rats increase and multiply and spread to other places, carrying disease and destruction.

✳   ✳   ✳

I find that it adds greatly to the interest of life to keep careful accounts of the business of housekeeping with its sidelines of poultry and small fruits.

Especially do the account books add a spice when the Man Of The Place gets angry because the hens get into the barn and scratch things around, or when the grain is getting low in the bins in the spring and he comes to you and says: "Those durn hens are eating their heads off!"

Then, if you can bring your little account book and show him that the feed for the hens cost so much, and the eggs and poultry sold brought so much, leaving a good little profit besides the eggs and poultry used in the house, he will feel better about things in general, and especially the hens.

A woman I know kept for one year the accounts of the household and her own especial little extra work and surprised herself by finding that by her own efforts she had made a clear profit of $395 during the year, and this without neglecting in any way her household or home duties.

The total for household expenses and her own personal expenses for the same time was $122.29. There is after all, you see, some excuse for the man who told a friend he was going to be married. "Be married!" the friend exclaimed, in surprise. "Why, you can't make a living for yourself!" To which the first man replied, sulkily: "Well, it's a pity if she can't help a little."

My friend proved that she could "help a little." Her books made such a good showing that her husband asked her to keep books for the farm and so she was promoted to the position of farm accountant (without salary).

Considering the amount of time, labor and capital invested, the farm books did not balance out so well as her own and she became interested in hunting the reason why. So now she has become a sort of farm adviser with who her husband consults on all matters of farm business.

We are told that the life of a woman on a farm is narrow and that the monotony of it drives many farm women insane. That life on a farm as elsewhere is just what we make it, that much and no more, is being proved every day by women who, like this one, pick up a thread connecting farm life with the whole, great outside world.

In the study of soils, of crops, their origin and proper cultivation and rotation; in the study of the livestock on the place, their proper selection and care; with the care of her house and poultry, always looking for a short cut in the work to gain time for some other interesting thing, there does not seem to be much chance for monotony to drive her insane.

That "all work and no play makes Jack a dull boy" is very true, I think. It is just as dull for Jill as it is for Jack, and so they formed a "Neighborhood Crochet club" down in "Happy Hollow." The women met and learned the new crochet patterns and visited——?——Well, gossiped, then——as the men do when they go to town on Saturday and have so much business (?) to attend to that they cannot get home until late chore time.

By the way, did you ever think that as much good can be done by the right kind of gossip as harm by the unkind sort? The Crochet club made a little play time mixed with the work all summer, until bad weather and the grippe interfered in the fall. Jill was not so dull and the plans are made for the club to meet again soon.

We do enjoy sitting around the fireplace in the evening and on stormy days in the winter.

When we planned our new house we determined that we would build the fireplace first and the rest of the house if we could afford it——not a grate, but a good old-fashioned fireplace that will burn a stick of wood as large as a man can carry. We have seen to it besides that there is a wood lot left on the farm to provide those sticks. So far we have escaped having the grippe, while all the neighborhood has been suffering with it. We attribute our good fortune to this same big fireplace and the two open stairs in the house. The fresh air they furnish has been much cheaper as well as much pleasanter to take than the doctor's medicine.

Some old-fashioned things like fresh air and sunshine are hard to beat. In our mad rush for progress and modern improvements let's be sure we take along with us all the old-fashioned things worth while.

The magazines say that the spring fashions will return to the styles of our grandmothers, ruffles, pantalettes, ribbon armlets and all. It will surely be delightful to have women's clothes soft and fluffy again and we need not follow the freak styles, you know. There is a distinct advantage in choosing the rather moderate, quiet styles for the up-to-the-minute freaks soon go out and then they call attention to their out-of-dateness by their striking appearance, while others equally as good style but not so pronounced will be a pleasure for more than one season.

So We Moved the Spring

How Running Water Was Provided for the Rocky Ridge Farm Home

There was once a farmer, so the story goes, who hauled water in barrels from a distant creek. A neighbor remonstrated with him for not digging a well and having his water supply handier. The farmer contended that he did not have time.

"But," said the neighbor, "the time you would save by not having to haul water would be more than enough to do the work."

"Yes, I know," replied the farmer, "but you see I am so busy hauling water that I can't get time to dig the well."

There is a story of another man who also had trouble in supplying his place with water. This man hauled water for half a mile.

"Why don't you dig a well," asked a stranger, "and not haul water so far?"
"Well," said the farmer, "it's about as fur to water one way as 'tis t'other."

I do not pretend to be the original discoverer of these stories, neither do I vouch for their truthfulness, but I do know that they correctly picture the fix we were in before we moved the spring.

We "packed water from the spring" for years at Rocky Ridge farm. Now and then when we were tired or in a special hurry, we would declare that something must be done about it. We would dig a well or build a cistern or something, the something being rather vague. At last, the "something" was what we did. Like the men in the stories we were too busy "packing water" to dig a well, and anyway it was "about as fur to water one way as t'other," so we decided to make an extra effort and move a spring. There were several never-failing springs on the farm but none of them were right at the house. We did not wish to move the house and besides it is very easy to move a spring, if one knows how, much easier than to move a house.

One trouble was to decide which spring. The one from which we carried water was nearest but it would require a ram to raise the water up to the house as the spring was in a gulch much lower than the buildings. Then, too, although it never went dry, it did run a little low during a dry spell. There were the three springs in the "Little Pasture." They ran strong enough but they also would require a ram to lift the water. We wished our water supply to be permanent and as little trouble to us as possible when once arranged, so we looked farther. Up on a hill in the pasture about 1,400 feet from the building was a spring which we had been watching for a year. The flow of water was steady, not seeming to be much affected by dry weather.

We found by using a level that this spring, at the head of a hollow in the hill, was enough higher than the hill where the buildings were situated to give the water a fall of 60 feet. We decided to move this spring and the Man Of The Place would do it with only common labor to help. The spring was dug out down to solid rock in the shape of a well, and a basin made in this a foot deep. In this well was built a cement reservoir 8 feet in diameter, the walls of which were 11 feet high, extending 3 feet above the surface of the ground. It holds about 30 barrels of water. A heavy cement cover in the form of an arch was placed over the top. It takes two men to lift it so that no one will look in from curiosity and leave the cover displaced. The cement was reinforced with heavy woven wire fence to make it strong. The walls and the cover are so thick and the shade of the oaks, elms and maples surrounding it is so dense that the water does not freeze in winter and is kept cool in summer. A waste pipe was laid in the cement six inches from the top of the reservoir to allow the surplus water to flow off if the reservoir should become overfull. It is in the nature of a water trap as the opening is beneath the surface of the water and both ends are covered with fine screen to prevent anything from entering the pipe.

The pipe that brings the water down to the buildings is in the lower side of the reservoir about a foot from the bottom. It was laid in the cement when the wall was built so that it is firmly embedded. The end which projects into the water was fitted with a drive well point, screened to keep out foreign substances and prevent sand and gravel from washing into the pipe. The pipe is laid 2 feet underground all the way to the buildings and grass grows thickly over it the for the whole distance. Because of this the water does not become heated while passing through in warm weather and there is no danger of its freezing and bursting the pipe in winter. The screen in the drive well point is brass and the pipes are heavily galvanized inside and out. There is, therefore, no taste of iron or rust added to the water. We have moved the spring so that it flows into a corner of the kitchen as pure as at its source.

We have multiplied our spring as well as moved it. We revel in water! There is a hydrant in the hen house, one in the barn, one in the calf lot, one in the garden and one at the back of the house, besides the faucets in the house. The supply of water is ample, for we tried it thoroly during a dry season. By attaching a hose to a hydrant, we can throw water over the top of the house or barn in a steady stream with the full force of a 60-foot fall and 30 barrels of water behind, so we feel we have protection in case of fire.

A man came out from town one day and after seeing the water works and drinking some of the water he exclaimed, "Why, this is better than living in town!"

We have saved more than time enough to dig a well but now we do not need to dig it so we find that time seems to run in doubles this way as well as the other.

We are told that "There is no great loss without some small gain." Even so I think that there is no great gain without a little loss. We do not carry water from the spring any more which is a very great gain, but it was sometimes pleasant to loiter by the way and that we miss a little.

Haying While the Sun Shines

One of the neighbors needed some help in the hay harvest. Being too busy to go himself, he called a town friend by telephone and asked him, if possible, to send out some one to work thru haying.

Mansfield has made a beautiful shady park of the public square in the center of town and it is the gathering place for those who have idle time on their hands. Everyone enjoys it, the busy man with just a few idle minutes as well as the town loafers who, perhaps, have a few busy minutes now and then. It seemed like a very good place to look for a man to help in the hay field, so here the obliging friend went.

"Any of you fellows want a job?" he asked a group resting in the shade. "Yes" said one man. "I do." "Work on a farm?" asked the friend. "Yes, for I need a job," was the reply. "Can you go out in the morning?" was the next question. "How far out is it?" asked the man who needed a job. "Two miles and a half," he was told. "Can't do it!" he exclaimed, dropping back into the restful position from which he had been disturbed. "I wouldn't go that far from town to work for anybody."

The Man Of The Place, inquiring in town for help, was told that it was not much use to look for it. "Jack was in the other day and begged with tears in his eyes for some one to come and help him get his hay and he couldn't get anyone." Jack's place is only half a mile from town so surely it could not be too far out, but to be sure the sun was shining rather warm in the hay field and the shade in the park was pleasanter. All of which reminds one of the tramp of whom Rose Wilder Lane tells in her Soldiers of the Soil. She met him, one of many, while on her walking tour thru the state of California. After listening to his tale of woe, she asked him why he did not look for work on a farm. She was sure there must be a chance of finding a job there, for the farmers were very short of help. To her suggestion the tramp replied, "Who wants to work like a farmer anyway!"

No one seems to want to "work like a farmer," except the farmer's wife. Well! Perhaps she does not exactly want to, but from the way she goes about it no one would suspect that she did not. In our neighborhood we are taking over more of the chores to give the men longer days in the field. We are milking the cows, turning the separator, feeding the calves and pigs and doing whatever else is possible, even going into the fields at times. Farmers are being urged to raise more food for the world consumption, to till more acres and also produce more to the acre. Their hands are quite full now and it seems that about the only way they could procure more help would be to marry more wives.

A few days ago I ran away from a thousand things waiting to be done and stole a little visit with a friend. And so I learned another way to cut across a corner and save work. Here it is, the way Mrs. Craig makes plum jelly. Cook the plums and strain out the juice: then to 3 cups of the boiling juice add 4 cups of sugar and stir until dissolved. Fill jelly glasses at once and set to one side. If the juice is fresh it will be jelled in the morning but if the juice is from canned plums it takes longer and may have to set over until the next day but it jells beautifully in the end.

A Dog's a Dog for a' That

INTELLIGENT PETS SOMETIMES SEEM ALMOST LIKE REAL FOLKS

Laura was very much a "dog person," and saw no reason to deny animals the emotional, and even moral qualities she often observed in them. In *Little House on the Prairie* she describes how Jack, the family bulldog, trotted behind the wagon all the way from Wisconsin to the Indian Territory. He was a loyal and helpful dog, and Laura describes his death touchingly in the second chapter of *By the Shores of Silver Lake*.

A redbird swinging in the grape arbor saw himself in the glass of my kitchen window not long ago. He tried to fly thru the glass to reach the strange bird he saw there and when his little mate came flitting by he tried to fight his reflection. Apparently he was jealous. During all one day he fretted and struggled to drive the stranger away. He must have told his little wife about it that night, I think, for in the morning they came to the arbor together and she alighted before the window while he stayed in the background. She gave Mr. Redbird one look, after glancing in the glass, then turned and flew fiercely at her reflection, twittering angrily. One could imagine her saying: "So that's it! This strange lady Redbird is the reason for your hanging around here instead of getting busy building the nest. I thought something was wrong, but I'll soon drive her away!" She tried to fight the strange lady until her husband objected to her paying so much attention to his rival and then they took turns, he declaring there was a gentleman there, she vowing there was a lady and doing her best to drive her away. At last between them they seemed to understand and now they both come occasionally to swing on the grape vine before the window and admire themselves in the glass.

* * *

There are many interesting things in the out-of-doors life that comes so close to us in the country, and if we show a little kindness to the wild creatures they quickly make friends with us and permit us a delightful intimacy with them and their homes. A bird in a cage is not a pretty sight, to me, but it is a pleasure to have the wild birds and the squirrels nesting around the house and so tame that they do not mind our watching them. Persons who shoot or allow shooting on their farms drive away a great deal of amusement and pleasure with the game, as well as do themselves pecuniary damage, while a small boy with a stone handy can do even more mischief than a man with a gun.

It is surprising how like human beings animals seem when they are treated with consideration. Did you ever notice the sense of humor animals have? Ever see a dog apologize—not a cringing fawning for favor, but a frank apology as one gentleman to another?

Shep was trying to learn to sit up and shake hands, but try as he would he could not seem to get the knack of keeping his balance in an upright position. He was an old dog and you know it has been said that, "It is hard to teach an old dog new tricks." No sympathy has ever been wasted on the dog but I can assure you that it also is hard for the old dog. After a particularly disheartening session one day, we saw him out on the back porch alone and not knowing that he was observed. He was practicing his lesson without a teacher. We watched while he tried and failed several times, then finally got the trick of it and sat up with his paw extended. The next time we said, "How do you do, Shep," he had his lesson perfectly. After that it was easy to teach him to fold his paws and be a "Teddy Bear" and to tell us what he said to tramps. We never asked him to lie down and roll over. He was not that kind of a character. Shep never would do his tricks for any one but us, tho he would shake hands with others when we told him to do so. His eyesight became poor as he grew older and he did not always recognize his friends. Once he made a mistake and barked savagely at an old friend whom he really regarded as one of the family tho he had not seen him for some time. Later as we all sat in the door yard, Shep seemed uneasy. Evidently there was something on his mind. At last he walked deliberately to the visitor, sat up and held out his paw. It was so plainly an apology that our friend said: "That's all right Shep old fellow! Shake and forget it!" Shep shook hands and walked away perfectly satisfied.

My little French Poodle, Incubus, is blind. He used to be very active and run abut the farm; but his chief duty, as he saw it, was to protect me. Altho he cannot see, he still performs that duty, guarding me at night and flying at any stranger who comes too near me during the day. Of what he is thinking, when he sits for long periods in the yard, with his face to the sun, I am too stupid to understand perfectly but I feel that in his little doggy heart, he is asking the eternal, "Why?" as we all do at times. After awhile he seemingly decides to make the best of it and takes a walk around the familiar places, or comes in the house and does his little tricks for candy with cheery good will. If patience and cheerfulness and courage, if being faithful to our trust and doing our duty under difficulties count for so much in man that he expects to be rewarded for them, both here and hereafter, how are they any less in the life of my little blind dog? Surely such virtues in animals are worth counting in the sum total of good in the universe.

An Autumn Day

Here Laura provides a quick summary of the things she loves about living in the country, and shares the philosophy that lets her put the dull business of daily chores in a proper perspective.

King Winter has sent warning of his coming! There was a delightful freshness in the air the other morning, and all over the low places lay the first frost of the season.

What a beautiful world this is! Have you noticed the wonderful coloring of the sky at sunrise? For me there is no time like the early morning, when the spirit of light broods over the earth at its awakening. What glorious colors in the woods these days! Did you ever think that great painters have spent their lives trying to reproduce on canvas what we may see every day? Thousands of dollars are paid for their pictures which are not so beautiful as those nature gives us freely. The colors in the sky at sunset, the delicate tints of the early spring foliage, the brilliant autumn leaves, softly colored grasses and lovely flowers—what painter ever equalled their beauties with paint and brush? I have in my living room three large windows uncovered by curtains which I call my pictures. Everchanging with the seasons, with wild birds and gay squirrels passing on and off the scene, I never have seen a landscape painting to compare with them.

As we go about our daily tasks the work will seem lighter if we enjoy these beautiful things that are just outside our doors and windows. It pays to go the top of the hill, now and then, to see the view and stroll thru the wood lot or pasture forgetting that we are in a hurry or that there is such a thing as a clock in the world. You are "so busy!" Oh yes I know it! We are all busy, but what are we living for anyway and why is the world so beautiful if not for us? The habits we form last us thru this life and I firmly believe into the next. Let's not make such a habit of hurry and work that when we leave this world we will feel impelled to hurry thru the spaces of the universe using our wings for feather dusters to clean away the star dust.

The true way to live is to enjoy every moment as it passes and surely it is in the everyday things around us that the beauty of life lies.

I strolled today down a woodland path—
A crow cawed loudly and flew away.
The sky was blue and the clouds were gold
And drifted before me fold on fold;
The leaves were yellow and red and brown
And patter, patter the nuts fell down,
On this beautiful, golden autumn day.

A squirrel was storing his winter hoard,
The world was pleasant: I lingered long.
The brown quails rose with a sudden whirr
And a little bundle, of eyes and fur,
Took shape of a rabbit and leaped away.
A little chipmunk came out to play
And the autumn breeze sang a wonder song.

According to Experts

Twenty-two years after writing this account of how the people of De Smet survived the abnormally harsh winter of 1880-81, Laura published *The Long Winter,* her book-length account of the ordeal. In chapter 19 of the book, "Where there's a Will," she describes how the Ingalls used a coffee mill to grind wheat and had to twist hay into "sticks" for fuel. The "two young men" who, when the town's wheat supply was all but exhausted, "dared to drive fifteen miles to where a solitary settler had also laid in his supply of seed wheat," were Laura's future husband Almanzo Wilder and his friend Cap Garland. The full story of their heroic journey is told in chapter 27 of *The Long Winter,* "For Daily Bread."

In a late issue of a St. Louis paper, I find the following: "Experts in the office of home economics of the United States Department of Agriculture have found it is possible to grind whole wheat in an ordinary coffee mill fine enough for use as a breakfast cereal and even fine enough for use in bread making."

If the experts of the Department of Agriculture had asked any one of the 200 people who spent the winter of 1880-81 in De Smet, S. Dak., they might have saved themselves the trouble of experimenting. I think, myself, that it is rather a joke on our experts at Washington to be 36 years behind the times.

That winter, known still among the old residents as "the hard winter," we demonstrated that wheat could be ground in an ordinary coffee mill and used for bread making. Prepared in that way it was the staff of life for the whole community. The grinding at home was not done to reduce the cost of living, but simply to make living possible.

De Smet was built as the railroad went thru, out in the midst of the great Dakota prairies far ahead of the farming settlements, and this first winter of its existence it was isolated from the rest of the world from December 1 until May 10 by the fearful blizzards that piled the snow 40 feet deep on the railroad tracks. The trains could not get thru. It was at the risk of life that anyone went even a mile from shelter, for the storms came up so quickly and were so fierce it was literally impossible to see the hand before the face and men have frozen to death within a few feet of shelter because they did not know they were near safety.

The small supply of provisions in town soon gave out. The last sack of flour sold for $50 and the last of the sugar at $1 a pound. There was some wheat on hand, brought in the fall before for seed in the spring, and two young men dared to drive 15 miles to where a solitary settler had also laid in his supply of seed wheat. They brought it in on sleds. There were no mills in town or country so this wheat was all ground in the homes in coffee mills, even the children taking their turns, and the resultant whole wheat flour made good bread. It was also a healthful food and there was not a case of sickness in town that winter.

It may be that the generous supply of fresh air had something to do with the general good health. Air is certainly fresh when the thermometer registers all the way from 15 to 40 degrees below zero with the wind moving at blizzard speed. In the main street of the town, snow drifts in one night were piled as high as the second stories of the houses and packed hard enough to drive over and the next night the wind might sweep the spot bare. As the houses were new and unfinished so that the snow would blow in and drift across us as we slept, fresh air was not a luxury. The houses were not overheated in daytime either, for the fuel gave out early in the winter and all there was left with which to cook and keep warm was the long prairie hay. A handful of hay was twisted into a rope, then doubled and allowed to twist back on itself and the two ends tied together in a knot, making what we called "a stick of hay."

It was a busy job to keep a supply of these "sticks" ahead of a hungry stove when the storm winds were blowing, but everyone took his turn good naturedly. There is something in living close to the great elemental forces of nature that causes people to rise above small annoyances and discomforts.

A train got thru May 10 and stopped at the station. All the men in town were down at the tracks to meet it, eager for supplies, for even the wheat had come to short rations. They found that what had been sent into the hungry town was a trainload of machinery. Luckily, there were also two emigrant cars well supplied with provisions, which were taken out and divided among the people. Our days of grinding wheat in coffee mills were over, but we had learned without expert aid that it can be done and that the flour so ground will make good bread and mush. Perhaps I would better say that we had all become experts and demonstrated the fact. After all necessity is the mother of invention and experience is a good old teacher.

Doing Our Best

I am proud of Marian because she is not a quitter; because she can take disappointment without a whimper and go bravely ahead with her undertakings even tho things do not always work out as she would like. I am sure, as the years pass, Marian will answer perfectly that good, old description of a lady, "Still mistress of herself tho china fall."

Marian failed to send her application in time to become a member of the *Ruralist* Poultry Club, but she is hustler nevertheless and should not be classed as being too slow to win in the race for membership. It was not really her fault, for the Missouri *Ruralist* does not come to her home, so she had not read about the club and as she is a little girl, only 10 years old, I did not tell her of the club until I had spent some time telling older girls about it. You see she did not have a fair start.

When she received word that the club membership was complete and her application was too late, the least that might have been expected was a crying spell, but not this little girl! She sat still a moment and then said quietly: "Well I'm going ahead just the same. Maybe some of the other girls will drop out and there will be a place for me, anyway I'll be learning how." She is keeping her record carefully and trying to reform a farm flock of egg-eating hens while she is waiting for her purebred Buff Orpingtons to grow up and take their place.

Many a grown person might learn a lesson from the way she took her disappointment. I am certainly proud of Marian.

"In the spring a young man's fancy lightly turns to thoughts of love," sings the poet, but in the spring the fancy of a hawk surely turns to spring chicken. Day after day he dines on the plumpest and fairest of the flock. I may spend half the day watching and never catch a glimpse of him then the moment my back is turned—swoop!—and he is gone with a chicken.

I should like to sentence that ex-governor who vetoed the state bounty on hawks to make his living raising chickens in the hills and not permit him to have a gun on the place, just by way of fitting the punishment to the crime. I know it is said that hawks are a benefit to the farmers because they catch field mice and other pests, but I am sure they would not look for a mouse if there were a flock of chickens near by. Even if they do catch mice, that is small comfort to the farmer's wife who loses half, or perhaps all her hatch of chicks, especially when she knows that the expense of feeding poultry is doubled because they dare not range the fields freely.

If there were enough of a bounty on hawks to make it an object to hunt them, farm women would surprise the food controller by the amount of poultry products they would put on the market. I believe the present output would be doubled if the hawks could be exterminated, for many a chicken dinner and dozens of eggs fly away on the wings of the hawks. At the price of eggs and dinners this is rather expensive and it is certainly discouraging to lose chicks that way after one has overcome all the other difficulties of their raising. I suppose tho that we will be as game as Marian and do the best we can under the circumstances. Doing the best we can is all that could be expected of us in any case, but did you ever notice how hard it is to do our best if we allow ourselves to become discouraged? If we are disheartened we usually lag in our efforts more or less. It is so easy to slump a little when we can give the blame to circumstances. I think Marian has found the way to overcome this by being so busy with mind and muscle at the work in hand that there is no time for thoughts of failure or for bemoaning our hard luck.

A Bouquet of Wild Flowers

Here Laura gives us a preview of the wonderful descriptions of nature in her Little House books. The "purple flags" (iris) that she describes here bloom again in chapter 3 of *On the Banks of Plum Creek,* where the walk to school is also mentioned. But even in such an Arcadian piece, Laura characteristically finds time to consider her theme in a broader context, in this case the Russian Revolution.

The Man of The Place brought me a bouquet of wild flowers this morning. It has been a habit of his for years. He never brings me cultivated flowers but always the wild blossoms of field and woodland and I think them much more beautiful.

In my bouquet this morning was a purple flag. Do you remember gathering them down on the flats and in the creek bottoms when you were a barefoot child? There was one marshy corner of the pasture down by the creek, where the grass grew lush and green; where the cows loved to feed and could always be found when it was time to drive them up at night. All thru the tall grass were scattered purple and white flag blossoms and I have stood in that peaceful grassland corner, with the red cow and the spotted cow and the roan cow taking their goodnight mouthfuls of the sweet grass, and watched the sun setting behind the hilltop and loved the purple flags and the rippling brook and wondered at the beauty of the world while I wriggled my bare toes down, into the soft grass.

The wild Sweet Williams in my bouquet brought a far different picture to my mind. A window had been broken in the schoolhouse at the country crossroads and the pieces of glass lay scattered where they had fallen. Several little girls going to school for their first term had picked handfuls of Sweet Williams and were gathered near the window. Someone discovered that the blossoms could be pulled from the stem and, by wetting their faces, could be stuck to the pieces of glass in whatever fashion they were arranged. They dried on the glass and would stay that way for hours and, looked at thru the glass, were very pretty. I was one of those little girls and tho I have forgotten what it was that I tried to learn out of a book that summer, I never have forgotten the beautiful wreaths and stars and other figures we made on the glass with the Sweet Williams. The delicate fragrance of their blossoms this morning made me feel like a little girl again.

The little white daisies with their hearts of gold grew thickly along the path where we walked to Sunday school. Father and sister and I used to walk the 2 ½ miles every Sunday morning. The horses had worked hard all the week and must rest this one day and Mother would rather stay at home with baby brother[11] so with Father and Sister Mary I walked to the church thru the beauties of the sunny spring Sundays. I have forgotten what I was taught on those days also. I was only a little girl, you know. But I can still plainly see the grass and the trees and the path winding ahead, flecked with sunshine and shadow and the beautiful golden-hearted daisies scattered all along the way.

Ah well! That was years ago and there have been so many changes since then that it would seem such simple things should be forgotten, but at the long last I am beginning to learn that it is the sweet, simple things of life which are the real ones after all.

We heap up around us things that we do not need as the crow makes piles of glittering pebbles. We gabble words like parrots until we lose the sense of their meaning; we chase after this new idea and that; we take any old thought and dress it out in so many words that the thought itself is lost in its clothing like a slim woman in a barrel skirt and then we exclaim, "Lo, the wonderful new thought I have found!"

"There is nothing new under the sun," says the proverb. I think the meaning is that there are just so many truths or laws of life and no matter how far we may think we have advanced we cannot get beyond those laws. However complex a structure we build of living we must come back to those truths and so we find we have traveled in a circle.

The Russian revolution[12] has only taken the people back to the democratic form of government they had at the beginning of history in medieval times and so a republic is nothing new. I believe we would be happier to have a personal revolution in our individual lives and go back to simpler living and more direct thinking. It is the simple things of life that make living worth while, the sweet fundamental things such as love and duty, work and rest and living close to nature. There are no hothouse blossoms that can compare in beauty and fragrance with my bouquet of wild flowers.

Are We Too Busy?

The sunlight and shadows in the woods were beautiful that morning, the sunlight a little pale and the air with that quality of hushed expectancy that the coming of autumn brings. Birds were calling to one another and telling of the wonderful Southland and the journey they must take before long. The whole, wide outdoors called me and tired muscles and nerves rasped from the summer's rush pleaded for rest, but there was pickle to make, drying apples to attend to, vegetables and fruits that must be gathered and stored, the Saturday baking and the thousands things of the everyday routine to be done.

"Oh, for a little time to enjoy the beauties around me," I thought. "Just a little while to be free of the tyranny of things that must be done!" A feeling of bitterness crept into my soul. "You'll have plenty of leisure some day when you are past enjoying it," I thought. "You know, in time, you always get what you have longed for and when you are old and feeble and past active use then you'll have all the leisure you ever have wanted. But my word! You'll not enjoy it!"

I was horrified at these thoughts, which almost seemed spoken to me. We do seem at times to have more than one personality, for as I gave a dismayed gasp at the prospect, I seemed to hear a reply in a calm, quiet voice.

"You need not lose your power of enjoyment nor your sense of the beautiful if you desire to keep them," it said. Keep the doors of your mind and heart open to them and your appreciation of such things will grow and you will be able to enjoy your well earned leisure when it comes even tho you should be older and not so strong. It is all in your own hands and may be as you wish."

We are all beginning to show the strain of the busy summer. Mrs. Menton has put up a full two years' supply of canned and dried fruits and vegetables. She says that, even tho no part of it should be needed to save anyone from starving, she will feel well repaid in the smallness of their grocery bills the coming year. She also confessed she was glad the lull in work was in sight for there wasn't "a whole pair of socks on the place."

Several women were comparing notes the other day. Said one, "My man says he doesn't mind a decent patch but he does hate to go around with a hole in his khakis." Everyone smiled understandingly and another took up the tale.

"Joe said this morning that he wished I'd make a working and call the neighbors in to fix up his clothes," she said, "but I told him you were all too busy to come."

There has been no time this summer to do the regular work properly. Mrs. Clearly said that if the rush of work does not stop soon she will have to stop anyway. She is a recent comer to the Ozarks and thru the dry seasons she has hoped for a good crop year. Now she does not know whether she will pray for rain next year or not. A good crop year does bring work with it and tho the worst may be over, there are still busy days ahead. There are the late fruits and garden truck to be put up, potato harvest and corn harvest, the second crop of timothy and clover and more cutting of alfalfa. There is the sorghum to make and the silos to fill and everything to be made snug for winter. Some of us will help in the actual work and others will be cooking for extra help. Whatever may be expected of us later, women have certainly done their utmost during this summer so nearly gone.

The Man of The Place and I have realized with something of the shock of a surprise that we do not need to buy anything during the coming year. There are some things we need and much that we would like to get but if it were necessary we could go very comfortably thru the year without a thing more than we now have on the place. There is wheat for our bread and potatoes, both Irish and sweet, there are beans and corn and peas. Our meat, milk, cream, butter and eggs are provided. A year's supply of fruit and sweetening are at hand and a plentiful supply of fuel in the woodlot. All this, to say nothing of the surplus.

During the summer when I have read of the high wages paid in factories and shops there has been a little feeling of envy in the back of my mind, but I suppose if those working people had had a year's supply of fuel and provisions and no rent to pay they would think it wonderful good fortune. After all, as the Irishman said, "Everything is evened up in this world. The rich buy their ice in the summer, but the poor get theirs in the winter."

The Man of The Place and I had known before that farmers are independent but we never had realized it and there is a difference between knowing and realizing. Have you realized it personally or do you just know in a general way? Thanksgiving will soon be here and it is time to be getting our blessings in order. But why wait for Thanksgiving? Why not just be thankful now?

Get the Habit of Being Ready

Laura's life as a pioneer had made her well-acquainted with the need to be prepared for emergencies, and there are many examples in the Little House books of Pa's and Ma's shrewdness in this regard. Here Laura shares her thoughts on the subject, and concludes, with pioneer fortitude, that "It does not so much matter what happens. It is what one does when it happens that really counts."

*D*id the first frost catch you unready? It would be quite unusual if it didn't because I never knew anyone to be ready for cold weather, in the fall, or for the first warm spell in the spring. It is like choosing the right time to be ill or an out-of-the-way place for a boil—it simply isn't done!

I know a man who had a little patch of corn. He was not quite ready to cut it and besides he said, "it is just a little green." He let it wait until the frost struck it and now he says it is too dry and not worth cutting. The frost saved him a lot of hard work.

This man's disposition reminds me of that of a renter we once had who was unable to plow the corn in all summer. Before it rained the ground was so hard he could not keep the plow in, and besides if it did not rain there would be no corn anyway and he believed it was going to be a dry season. When it did rain it was too wet to plow and never was he ready and able to catch that cornfield when the ground was right for plowing.

And that reminds me of the other renter who was always ready to take advantage of his opportunities. His horses would break into the cornfield at night, or were turned in (we never knew which), and in the fall, when The Man Of The Place wanted a share of what corn was left, he was told that the horses had eaten all his share.

The anecdotes are not intended as any reflection on renters. I could tell some in which the joke is on the other side if I had the space.

The tragedy of being unready is easy to find for, more often than not, success or failure turn upon just that one thing. There was a time, perhaps long ago, when you were not ready for examinations and failed to pass, then there was the time you were not ready to make that good investment because you had been spending carelessly. We can all remember many times when we were not ready. While being ready for and equal to whatever comes may be in some sense a natural qualification, it is a characteristic that may be cultivated, especially if we learn easily by experience.

It was interesting to see the way different persons showed their character after the first frost. One man considered that the frost had done his work for him and so relieved him of further effort. Others went along at their usual gait and saved their fodder in a damaged condition. They had done the best they could, let providence take the responsibility. Still others worked thru the moonlight nights and saved their feed in good condition in spite of the frost. They figured that it "was up to them" and no little thing like the first frost should spoil their calculations.

It does not so much matter what happens. It is what one does when it happens that really counts.

Make a New Beginning

We should bring ourselves to an accounting at the beginning of the New Year and ask these questions: What have I accomplished? Where have I fallen short of what I desired and planned to do and be?

I never have been in favor of making good resolutions on New Year's Day just because it was the first day of the year. Any day may begin a new year for us in that way, but it does help some to have a set time to go over the year's efforts and see whether we are advancing or falling back.

If we find that we are quicker of temper and sharper of tongue than we were a year ago, we are on the wrong road. If we have less sympathy and understanding for others and are more selfish than we used to be, it is time to take a new path.

I helped a farmer figure out the value of his crops raised during the last season, recently, and he was a very astonished person. Then when we added to that figure the amount he had received for livestock during the same period, he said: "It doesn't seem as if a man who had taken in that much off his farm would need a loan."

This farmer friend had not kept any accounts and so was surprised at the money he had taken in and that it should all be spent. Besides the help in a business way, there are a great many interesting things that can be gotten out of farm accounts, if they are rightly kept.

The Man of The Place and I usually find out something new and unexpected when we figure up the business at the end of the year. We discovered this year that the two of us, without any outside help, had produced enough in the last year to feed 30 persons for a year—all the bread, butter, meat, eggs, sweetening and vegetables necessary—and this does not include the beef cattle sold off the place.

I do not know whether Mr. Hoover would think we have done as much as we should, but I do think it is not so bad. I had been rather discouraged with myself because I have not had so much time to spend with Red Cross work as some of my friends in town, but after I found out just what we have done, I felt better about it.

The knitting and making of garments for the Red Cross[13] is very necessary and important but the work of making the hens lay and filling the cream can is just as commendable. Without the food which the farm women are helping to produce,[14] the other work would be of no value.

If you have not already done so, just figure up for yourselves and you will be surprised at how much you have accomplished.

Make Your Dreams Come True

Now is the time to make a garden! Anyone can be a successful gardener at this time of year and I know of no pleasanter occupation these cold, snowy days, than to sit warm and snug by the fire making garden with pencil, in a seed catalog. What perfect vegetables do we raise in that way and so many of them! Our radishes are crisp and sweet, our lettuce tender and our tomatoes smooth and beautifully colored. Best of all, there is not a bug or worm in the whole garden and the work is so easily done.

In imagination we see the plants in our spring garden, all in straight, thrifty rows with the fruits of each plant and vine numerous and beautiful as the pictures before us. How near the real garden of next summer approaches the ideal garden of our winter fancies depends upon how practically we dream and how we work.

It is so much easier to plan than it is to accomplish. When I started my small flock of Leghorns a few years ago, a friend inquired as to the profits of the flock and taking my accounts as a basis, he figured I would be a millionaire within five years. The five years are past, but alas, I am still obliged to be economical. There was nothing wrong with my friend figuring, except that he left out the word "if" and that made all the difference between profits figured out on paper and those worked out by actual experience.

My Leghorns would have made me a millionaire—if the hens had performed according to schedule; if the hawks had loved field mice better than spring chickens; if I had been so constituted that I never became weary; if prices—but why enumerate? Because allowance for that word "if" was not made in the figuring, the whole result was wrong.

It is necessary that we dream now and then. No one ever achieved anything, from the smallest object to the greatest, unless the dream was dreamed first, yet those who stop at dreaming never accomplish anything. We must first see the vision in order to realize it; we must have the ideal or we cannot approach it; but when once the dream is dreamed it is time to wake up and "get busy." We must "do great deeds; not dream them all day long."

The dream is only the beginning. We'd starve to death if we went no further with that garden than making it by the fire in the seed catalog. It takes judgment to plant the seeds at the right time, in the right place, and hard digging to make them grow, whether in the vegetable garden or in the garden of our lives. The old proverb says, "God helps the man who helps himself," and I know that success in our undertakings can be made into a habit.

We can work our dreams out into realities if we try, but we must be willing to make the effort. Things that seem easy of accomplishment in dreams require a lot of good common sense to put on a working basis and a great deal of energy to put thru to a successful end. When we make our dream gardens we must take into account the hot sun and the blisters on our hand; we must make allowances for and guard against the "ifs" so that when the time to work has come they will not be of so much importance.

We may dream those dreams of a farm of our own; of a comfortable home; of that education we are going to have and those still more excellent dreams of the brotherhood of man and liberty and justice for all; then let us work to make this "the land where dreams come true."

Visit "Show You" Farm

There is at least one Missourian who is not asking to be "shown." A.C. Barton of Show You Farm says Missouri people have said "show me" long enough and they should now say "I will show you," which he is proceeding to do.

Mr. Barton used to be a Methodist preacher. He says that no one ever accused him of being the best preacher at the St. Louis conference, but they did all acknowledge that he was the best farmer among them. He thought perhaps he had made a mistake like the man who saw, in a vision, the letters G.P.C. and thought he had a call to preach, the letters standing for "Go Preach Christ." Later he decided the letters meant "Go Plow Corn," so Mr. Barton made up his mind to follow the profession in which he excelled. He came to Mountain Grove from Dallas county, Nebraska, 8 years ago.

While waiting for his train in Kansas City, Mr. Barton noticed a man, also waiting, surrounded by bundles and luggage. For some reason Mr. Barton thought he was from the Ozarks and approaching him asked:

"Are you from Missouri?"

"Yes sir," the man replied.

"From the Ozarks?" Mr. Barton inquired.

"Yes sir," answered the man.

"Are there any farms for sale down there where you came from?" Mr. Barton asked.

"Yes sir. They're all for sale," replied the man from the Ozarks.

While that might have been true at the time, it would not be true now, for Show You Farm is not for sale.

When Mr. Barton bought his 80-acre farm on the "post oak[15] flats" near Mountain Grove, the people he met gave him the encouragement usually given the new comers in the Ozarks. They told him the land was good for nothing, that he could not raise anything on it.

One man remarked in his hearing, "These new comers are workers," and another replied: "They'll have to work if they make a living on that place. Nobody's ever done it yet."

So "everybody works" and "father." The proprietors of Show You Farm are A.C. Barton, Nora L. Barton and family.

They soon found there was more work on an 80-acre farm than they could handle, for while there were eight in the family, the six children were small, so it was decided to adjust the work to the family and 40 acres of the land, on which were the improvements, were sold for $2,500. Later 15 acres more were sold for $600. As the place had cost only $40 an acre that left only $100 as the cost of the 25-acre farm that was kept.

These 25 acres of unimproved, poor land have been made into a truly remarkable little farm. During last season it produced the following crops: Ten acres of corn, 400 bushels; 2 acres of oats, 80 bushels; 1 acre of millet hay, 2 tons; 1 acre of sorghum, 115 gallons of molasses; cowpeas, 100 bushels. Besides these crops there was a 5-acre truck patch which furnished a good income thru the summer, but of which no account was kept. There has been sold off the place this last season livestock amounting to $130, poultry $15, butter $250, and grain $35. The rest of the grain was still on the place when this was written. Not bad for a 25-acre farm, is it?

As there is a young orchard of 3 acres, a pasture of 3 acres and necessarily some ground used for building sites, you may wonder where the cowpeas were raised. Mr. Barton plants cowpeas with all other crops. He says it is the surest, quickest and cheapest way to build up the soil. When garden crops are harvested cowpeas are planted in their place, they follow the oats and rye and are planted with the corn.

There never has been a pound of commercial fertilizer used on Show You Farm. When clearing his land, Mr. Barton traded wood for stable manure in the town, so that he paid, with his labor, for 300 tons of stable fertilizer. Except for this, the soil has been built up by rotation of crops and raising cowpeas, until from a complete failure of the corn crop the first year, because of poverty of the soil, last year's bountiful crops were harvested.

By the good farming methods of the Barton family they made their land bring them an average of $30 an acre even in the last dry seasons.

Mr. Barton believes in cultivation, both with plows and by hand. He is old fashioned enough to hoe his corn. A neighbor passing and seeing him hoeing said, "If I can't raise corn without hoeing it I won't raise it," and he didn't for it was a dry season. As Mr. Barton says, "The reason there are so many POOR farmers is because there are so many poor FARMERS." For the last four years Show You Farm has taken the blue ribbon for general farm exhibit at the Tri-county Stock Show at Mountain Grove and never less than eight blue ribbons in all.

The Barton children have no idea of leaving the farm. They are too much interested in their business for they are full partners with their parents. Mr. Barton says it is easy to interest children in the farm. All that is necessary is to talk to them about the work as it is going on and let them help to plan.

When he is planting the crops he plans with them about the results. "Let's figure it," he will say. "If we plant a hill of cantaloupes every 4 feet, we ought to raise two on every hill and if we sell them for 5 cents each that will bring us $128 an acre. But we should do better than that, we ought to make them bring us $300 an acre." And by explaining to them how to do this they are interested and eager to see how much they can make. The children work better when they are interested, Mr. Barton says, and they are willing to stay on the farm.

It is not all work and money making at the Barton home, however. In strawberry time the Sunday school is invited out and treated to strawberries with cream and sugar. Last season it took 8 gallons of strawberries to supply the feast. When melons are ripe there is another gathering and sometimes as many as 100 persons enjoy the delicious treat.

In the long winter evenings work and pleasure are mixed and while one of the family reads aloud some interesting book, the others shell the cowpeas that have been gathered in the fall.

Mr. Barton has not been allowed to drop all his outside activities. He has been elected secretary of the Farmers Mutual Fire Insurance Company and is helping them to organize for their mutual benefit. Also his services are often in demand to supply a country pulpit here and there, for once a Methodist preacher a man is always more or less a Methodist preacher, and as Mr. Barton goes on his daily way, both by acts and words, he is preaching kindness, helpfulness and the brotherhood of man.

He also preaches an agricultural theology. He says that robbing the soil is a sin, the greatest agricultural sin, and that like every other sin it brings its own punishment.

That Mr. Barton has not committed that sin, one is assured when looking over the farm and what he has accomplished is certainly encouraging for the man with a bit of poor land. Mr. Barton's advice to such a man is "not to go looking for a better place but MAKE one."

The Barton farmstead is built on rather an original plan. The house is 38 by 24 feet, with a kitchen at the back, 12x14 feet. Joining the back porch of this kitchen is a concrete store room 12x12 feet with the well in a corner, and joining this store room is a long shed 44x56 feet. This is all under one roof and is 170 feet long. It is planned to soon build a barn beyond and joining the shed. It will then be 200 feet from the front door to the back and visitors will be welcome all the way.

Make Every Minute Count

Spring has come! The wild birds have been singing the glad tidings for several days, but they are such optimistic little souls that I always take their songs of spring with a grain of pessimism. The squirrels and chipmunks have been chattering to me, telling me the same news, but they are such cheerful busybodies that I never believe quite all they say.

But now I know that spring is here for as I passed the little creek, on my way to the mail box this morning, I saw scattered papers caught on the bushes, empty cracker and sandwich cartons strewn around on the green grass and discolored pasteboard boxes soaking in the clear water of the spring. I knew then that spring was here, for the sign of the picnickers is more sure than that of singing birds and tender green grass, and there is nothing more unlovely than one of nature's beauty spots defiled in this way. It is such an unprovoked offense to nature, something like insulting one's host after enjoying his hospitality. It takes just a moment to put back into the basket the empty boxes and papers and one can depart gracefully leaving the place all clean and beautiful for the next time or the next party.

Did you ever arrive all clean and fresh, on a beautiful summer morning, at a pretty picnic place, and find that someone had been before you and that the place was all littered up with dirty papers and buzzing flies? If you have and have ever left a place in the same condition, it served you right. Let's keep the open spaces clean, not fill them up with rubbish!

It is so easy to get things cluttered up, one's days for instance, as well as picnic places—to fill them with empty, useless things and so make them unlovely and tiresome. Even tho the things with which we fill our days were once important, if they are serving no good purpose now, they have become trash like the empty boxes and papers of the picnickers. It will pay to clean this trash away and keep our days as uncluttered as possible.

There are just now so many things that must be done that we are tempted to spend ourselves recklessly, especially as it is rather difficult to decide what to eliminate, and we cannot possibly accomplish everything. We must continually be weighing and judging and discarding things that are presented to us, if we would save ourselves, and spend our time and strength only on those that are important. We may be called upon to spend our health and strength to the last bit, but we should see to it that we do not waste them.

"Oh I am so tired that I just want to sit down and cry," a friend confided to me, "and here is the club meeting on hand and the lodge practice and the Red Cross work day and the aid society meeting and the supper at the school house and the spring sewing and garden and—Oh! I don't see how I'm ever going to get thru with it all!"

Of course she was a little hysterical. It didn't all have to be done at once, but it showed how over-tired she was and it was plain that something must give way—if nothing else, herself. My friend needed a little open space in her life.

We must none of us shirk. We must do our part in every way, but let's be sure we clear away the rubbish, that we do nothing for empty form's sake nor because someone else does, unless it is the thing that should be done.

1. Almanzo and Laura moved from De Smet, South Dakota, to Mansfield, Missouri, in 1984.

2. Apple growing was a big business in Missouri when Almanzo and Laura started their orchard, as the following *Ruralist* article from the front page of the November 30, 1912, issue makes clear:

> "Missouri apples have always been in great demand. Every time a person outside Missouri gets a taste of one he wants another. The exclusive hotels in New York City must always have the best, so this year are buying them from an enterprising fruit grower in Laclede County, Missouri for fifteen cents apiece in the orchard … Each apple is carefully selected, clipped from the tree together with its stem and two perfect leaves, and packed and sealed in a separate box bearing the name and address of the grower. Combining flavor, quality and color such as can only be found in a Missouri apple, each,—Nature's closet approach to perfection,—will be served to wealthy New Yorkers in its original box with its seal unbroken for FORTY CENTS APIECE! That's some price, but isn't a Missouri apple worth it?"

3. Ben Davis—synonyms: Baltimore Pippin, Red Streak, Red Pippin, Victoria Red, etc.

> "This apple is of unknown origin. It was extensively planted in Virginia, Kentucky, Arkansas and the adjoining states at the beginning of the Civil War, and during the last thirty years has been disseminated throughout all the apple growing portions of the United States. From the first it has been exceedingly popular as a market apple, and is today unquestionably the leading commercial sort.... It is a showy apple, being large, symmetrical, and highly colored."
>
> —Charles T. Dearing, "Missouri's Best Dozen Apples"
> Missouri *Ruralist,* January 29, 1911

4. Missouri Pippin—synonyms: Missouri Keeper, Missouri Orange.

> "The Missouri Pippin is still another popular Missouri apple which has its origin here. Its home is Kingsville in Johnson county. It was disseminated throughout Missouri, Kansas and Illinois, shortly after the Civil War and has been a favorite of both growers and sellers ever since... The fruit of the Missouri Pippin is of medi-

um size, roundish, and has one side more developed than the other… Like the Ben Davis the skin is tough, smooth, glossy and waxy, but it differs in color, being pale-green or yellow, overspread with bright red, striped with deep purplish-red.

> —Charles T. Dearing, "Missouri's Best Dozen Apples"
> Missouri *Ruralist,* January 29, 1911

5. Whether the article was written exclusively by Almanzo, as the by-line suggests, or by Almanzo and Laura together, or even by Laura herself, cannot now be determined. However, since Laura's first *Ruralist* article ("Favors the Small Farm Home") had been published, prominently and under her own name, only four months earlier, there seems to be no obvious reason why this story, if written solely by her, should not also have been published under her own name.

6. Earlier in the year the state of Missouri had passed a law allowing farm names to be registered, and in response the *Ruralist* had organized a competition for stories in which readers described how, and why, their farms had been named. Four prizes were offered, as follows:

FIRST—One Climax Phonograph (made by the Columbian Phonograph Co.) and one dozen records, value $25.

SECOND—One D. & C. Merriam's latest edition Webster's Unabridged Dictionary, value $12.

THIRD—One dinner set—Royal Avenir Blue Dishes—43 pieces.

FOURTH—One Ladies' Gun Metal Watch.

For the period, these were generous prizes: a wood- or coal-burning stove could then be bought for $9, and an elaborate kitchen range for $19.

7. The article was distinguished from those of the winning contestants by being printed with a page-wide headline in display type and with a large photograph captioned: "A little of the 'Selvage Edge' At Rocky Ridge—the Hillside Above the Spring."

8. *Sorghum bicolor* (L.) Moench Subglabrescens group of cultivars; formerly *S. vulgare* Persoon, var. *subglabrescens* (von Steudel) A.F.Hill; matures earlier than Kafir.

9. *Sorghum bicolor (L.)* Moench, Caffrorum group of cultivars; formelry *S. vulgare Persoon,* var. *caffrorum* (Retzius) F.T. Hubbard & Rehder.

10. *Vigna unguiculata* (L.) Walpers.

11. Charles Frederick Ingalls, born November 1, 1875, died August 27, 1876.

12. Laura wrote this while the revolutionary but relatively moderate Menshevik government still ruled Russia. The October Revolution, which brought Trotsky, Lenin, and the Bolsheviks to power, was still some three and a half months away.

13. The Red Cross distributed such clothing to American soldiers in Europe; Laura worked for the Red Cross throughout World War I.

14. As part of the war effort on the home front.

15. *Quercus stellata* Wangenheim. Also called Iron Oak.

Making a Home

Favors the Small Farm Home

IT LESSENS THE INVESTMENT, IMPROVES COUNTRY SOCIAL CONDITIONS,
MAKES THE OWNER MORE INDEPENDENT OF POOR HELP, PROMOTES BETTER
FARMING METHODS AND REDUCES THE LABOR OF HOUSEKEEPING

This was Laura's first published article, originally written as an address to a local farmer's club meeting. (Laura, being a famous raiser of poultry, was much in demand at these events.) On this occasion, though, she was too busy to give the speech herself, and so she sent the text along for someone else to read. The editor of the Missouri *Ruralist,* John Francis Case, was in the audience, and liked what he heard. He decided to publish the article, and got in touch with Laura. And so her life as a writer began. Curiously enough, this very first article touches on several themes that preoccupied Laura throughout her career with the *Ruralist,* and that later appeared in the Little House books. First, she praises the virtue of rural life, especially for children. Then she suggests various practical ways to make country living easier and more attainable. She emphasizes the need for a real and equal partnership between a man and a woman. She advocates the use of modern labor-saving devices. She stresses the need for those who live in the country to keep in touch with modern developments, via newspapers (easily obtained through the Rural Free Delivery system) and through books (also easily available, courtesy of the Circulating Library system). She urges her readers to broaden their horizons, to make use of the new interurban trolley cars (soon to be powered, she foresees, by Missouri's readily available hydroelectric power), and to enrich their social and cultural lives by joining local clubs and organizations.

There is a movement in the United States today, wide-spread, and very far reaching in its consequences. People are seeking after a freer, healthier, happier life. They are tired of the noise and dirt, bad air and crowds of the cities and are turning longing eyes toward the green slopes, wooded hills, pure running water and health-giving breezes of the country.

A great many of these people are discouraged by the amount of capital required to buy a farm and hesitate at the thought of undertaking a new business. But there is no need to buy a large farm. A small farm will bring in a good living with less work and worry and the business is not hard to learn.

In a settlement of small farms the social life can be much pleasanter than on large farms, where the distance to the nearest neighbor is so great. Fifteen or twenty families on five acre farms will be near enough together to have pleasant social gatherings in the evenings. The women can have their embroidery clubs, their reading club and even the children can have their little parties, without much trouble or loss of time. This could not be done if each family lived on a 100 or 200-acre farm. There is less hired help required on the small farm also, and this makes the work in the house lighter.

I am an advocate of the small farm and I want to tell you how an ideal home can be made on, and a good living made from, five acres of land.

Whenever a woman's home-making is spoken of, the man in the case is presupposed and the woman's home-making is expected to consist in keeping the house clean and serving good meals on time, etc. In short, that all of her home-making should be inside the house. It takes more than the inside of the house to make a pleasant home and women are capable of making the whole home, outside and in, if necessary. She can do so to perfection on a five-acre farm by hiring some of the outside work done.

However, our ideal home should be made by a man and a woman together. First, I want to say that a five-acre farm is large enough for the support of a family. From $75 to $150 a month, besides a great part of the living can be made on that size farm from poultry or fruit or a combination of poultry, fruit and dairy.

This has been proved by actual experience so that the financial part of this small home is provided for.

Conditions have changed so much in the country within the last few years that we country women have no need to envy our sisters in the city. We women on the farm no longer expect to work as our grandmothers did.

With the high prices to be had for all kinds of timber and wood we now do not have to burn wood to save the expense of fuel, but can have our oil stove, which makes the work so much cooler in the summer, so much lighter and cleaner. There need be no carrying in of wood and carrying out of ashes, with the attendant dirt, dust and disorder.

Our cream separator saves us hours formerly spent in setting and skimming milk and washing pans, besides saving the large amount of cream that was lost in the old way.

Then there is the gasoline engine. Bless it! Besides doing the work of a hired man outside, it can be made to do the pumping of the water and the churning, turn the washing machine and even run the sewing machine.

On many farms running water can be supplied in the house from springs by means of rams or air pumps and I know of two places where water is piped into and through the house from springs farther up on the hills. This water is brought down by gravity alone and the only expense is the piping. There are many such places in the Ozark hills waiting to be taken advantage of.

This, you see, supplies water works for the kitchen and bath room simply for the initial cost of putting in the pipes. In one farm home I know, where there are no springs to pipe the water from, there is a deep well and a pump just outside the kitchen door. From this a pipe runs into a tank in the kitchen and from this tank there are two pipes. One runs into the cellar and the other underground to a tank in the barnyard, which is of course much lower than the one in the kitchen.

When water is wanted down cellar to keep the cream and butter cool a cork is pulled from the cellar pipe by means of a little chain and by simply pumping the pump outdoors, cold water runs into the vat in the cellar. The water already there rises and runs out at the overflow pipe, through the cellar and out at the cellar drain.

When the stock at the barn need watering, the cork is pulled from the other pipe and the water flows from the tank in the kitchen into the tank in the yard. And always the tank in the kitchen is full of fresh, cold water, because this other water all runs through it. This is a simple, inexpensive contrivance for use on a place where there is no running water.

It used to be that the woman on a farm was isolated and behind the times. A weekly paper was what the farmer read and he had to go to town to get that. All this is changed. Now the rural delivery brings us our daily papers and we keep up on the news of the world as well or better than though we lived in the city. The telephone gives us connection with the outside world at all times and we know what is going on in our nearest town by many a pleasant chat with our friends there.

Circulating libraries, thanks to our state university, are scattered through the rural districts and we are eagerly taking advantage of them.

The interurban trolley lines being built through our country will make it increasingly easy for us to run into town for an afternoon's shopping or any other pleasure. These trolley lines are and more will be, operated by electricity, furnished by our swift running streams, and in a few years our country homes will be lighted by this same electric power.

Yes indeed, things have changed in the country and we have the advantages of city life if we care to take them. Besides we have what it is impossible for the woman in the city to have. We have a whole five acres for our back yard and all outdoors for our conservatory, filled not only with beautiful flowers, but with grand old trees as well, with running water and beautiful birds, with sunshine and fresh air and all wild, free, beautiful things.

The children, instead of playing with other children in some street or alley can go make friends with the birds, on their nests in the bushes, as my little girl used to do, until the birds are so tame they will not fly at their approach. They can gather berries in the garden and nuts in the woods and grow strong and healthy, with rosy cheeks and bright eyes. This little farm home is a delightful place for friends to come for afternoon tea under the trees. There is room for a tennis court for the young people. There are skating parties in the winter and the sewing and reading clubs of the nearby towns, as well as the neighbor women, are always anxious for an invitation to hold their meetings there.

In conclusion I must say if there are any country women who are wasting their time envying their sisters in the city—don't do it. Such an attitude is out of date. Wake up to your opportunities. Look your place over and if you have not kept up with the modern improvements and conveniences in your home, bring yourself up to date. Then take the time saved from bringing water from the spring, setting the milk in the old way and churning by hand, to build yourself a better social life. If you don't take a daily paper subscribe for one. They are not expensive and are well worth the price in the brightening they will give your mind and the pleasant evenings you can have reading and discussing the news of the world. Take advantage of the circulating library. Make your little farm home noted for its hospitality and the social times you have there. Keep up with the march of progress for the time is coming when the cities will be the workshops of the world and abandoned to the workers, while the real cultured, social and intellectual life will be in the country.

Village Life the Solution

PROF. BAILEY FAVORS THE HAPPY MEDIUM
FOR SOLVING PRESENT PROBLEMS

$\mathcal{P}$rof. Liberty H. Bailey,[1] who was a member of President Roosevelt's Farm Commission and is one of the leading authorities of the country on rural questions, is quoted in a recent news dispatch as saying that much of our "back to the farm efforts" are misdirected. He favors the happy medium of an increased village life—a relief from the congestion of the cities and at the same time from the isolation of the country.

The real solution of present day living problems, Professor Bailey believes, is to get the people back to the villages. Manufacturing establishments should be kept away from the large cities and built in small towns where land is cheap and where every workman can have his own family garden to supply his table with vegetables, his own fruit trees, his own cow and unlimited quantities of pure air.

There has been a decline of comparative rural population since 1790, he said, when nine-tenths of the people were on farms. The present census showed that not more than one-fourth lived on the farms, and he believed that in 1920 not more than one-fifth would be on the farms.

Outdoor Life the Remedy

A *Ruralist* Report

Dr. Wiley, the food expert, states that drugs, drink and worry are making us a nation of nervous wrecks, and declares that practically every man and woman are at some time in their lives on the verge of insanity. Outdoor life is the remedy he suggests as the best cure for this condition.

Making the Best of Things

We would all be delighted to have modern kitchens, with up-to-date utensils; but some of us must put up with the old things while we are helping to pay off the mortgage or to save toward buying that little place of our own. However, we need not always use the old things in just exactly the old way; and sometimes we can even do better with a skillful juggling of our old tools than we could with some new fashioned utensil.

For instance, the woman who wishes she had a roaster so she would not be obliged to baste the roasting meat, may take two iron dripping pans, bend the handles of one pan a little narrower so they will slip through the handles of the other, and join them in that way with the roast inside. If she has poured a cup of hot water over the meat as she put it in the pan, she will not have to baste it.

The same pans used in the same way make a covered baking pan for light bread. The loaves cannot run over nor crack along the sides as they often do if baked in an open pan, and the crust is more tender and a more even brown. These pans may be separated in a second's time and used for anything else, and still become a roaster or baking pan at any time.

The idea of covering things may be carried farther and do away with some of the standing over a hot stove. When frying meat cover the skillet with a close cover. It will keep the grease from spattering over the stove, the meat will only require turning once, and it will be more tender. Do the same when frying eggs and they will not need to be turned, nor to have the hot grease dipped on them. They will cook much quicker and on both top and bottom. Chicken can be fried in the roasting pans and will brown evenly all over, without turning, if there is plenty of lard or butter in the pan.

If you wish to make some cheese and have no press, the lard press will do exactly as well. If you need the little kitchen table with the large wheel which you often see described for carrying loads of things from stove to table and from table to pantry, remember that any small table with large casters will do equally well and be much less expensive.

We may not be able to have electric lights, but we may have a much better light from our coal oil lamps and make the care of them easier by using them properly. The simple expedient of turning a lamp down before blowing it out will make the difference between a bright, clean burner with a good light and a burner that is dark and greasy, so causing a poor light with a bad odor. The wick acts as a pump to bring the oil to the blaze. As long as it is warm it keeps right on pumping. If the blaze is not there to burn it the oil overflows onto the outside of the burner, making a dirty lamp and a poor light.

Magic in Plain Foods

ALL THE WORLD SERVES A WOMAN WHEN SHE TELEPHONES

This is the second of two articles that Laura wrote for the *Ruralist* about the great San Francisco World's Fair. In it she dwells on the marvellous food and food-production exhibits, and relays to her readers a selection of ethnic recipes.

The thought came to me, while I wandered among the exhibits in the Food Products building at the San Francisco exposition, that Aladdin with his wonderful lamp had no more power than the modern woman in her kitchen. She takes down the receiver to telephone her grocery order, and immediately all over the world the monstrous genii of machinery are obedient to her command. All the nations of the world bring their offerings to her door—fruits from South America, Hawaii, Africa; tea and spices from India, China and Japan; olives and oil from Italy; coffee from strange tropical islands; sugar from Cuba and the Philippines.

This modern magic works both ways. The natives of all these far away places may eat the flour made from the wheat growing in the fields outside our kitchen windows. I never shall look at Missouri wheat fields again without thinking of the "Breads of All Nations" exhibit, where natives of eight foreign nations in the national costume were busy making the breads of their countries from our own American flour.

We use raisins, flour, tea, breakfast food, and a score of other common things without a thought of the modern miracles that make it possible for us to have them. For instance, who would have thought that different varieties of wheat are blended to make fine flour, just as a blend of coffee is used to make a perfect beverage? An entire flour mill, running and producing flour for the market, in the Food Products building, illustrates this fact. In California mills, California, Washington, Idaho, and Kansas wheat is blended according to scientific tests for the proper amount of gluten and starch. It is interesting to note that although this flour is not shipped east of the Rockies, because of the high freight rate, Kansas wheat is shipped west to make it.

One has a greater feeling of respect for the flour used daily, after seeing the infinite pains taken to turn out the perfect article. Every shipment of wheat to these mills, after being tested in the laboratories, is cleaned by a vacuum cleaner, ground through rollers and sifted, and then re-ground and re-sifted four times. During this process the finest, first grade flour is taken out, being sifted through 14 screens of fine, sheer silk. This first grade flour is kept for home use, the second grade being shipped to the Orient, where some of our middle-western wheat makes its final appearance as Chinese noodles.

From the time the wheat is poured into the hoppers until, in our kitchens, we cut the string that ties the sack, the flour is not exposed to the outer air. It is not touched by human hands until we dip the flour sifter into it. After the siftings the flour, still enclosed, passes through a machine which automatically removes a small sample every half hour, to be inspected by the miller. From this machine it goes into a compartment where it is purified by a current of filtered air, then it enters the chute which fills the sacks.

The output of this modern machine, handled by one man, is 400 sacks of flour and 125 sacks of bran, shorts and middlings every 24 hours. With the machinery in use 10 years ago, 10 or 12 men were required to produce the same amount.

Ten years ago, too, we seeded our raisings by hand ourselves, or bribed the children to the task by giving them a share to eat. Today we buy seeded raisins in boxes, without giving a thought to how the seeding is done. You may be sure of this—these package raisins are clean. They are scientifically clean, sterilized by steam and packed hot. In the Food Products building I saw these machines at work. This is the process:

Sun-dried Muscat grapes are stemmed by machinery, then sent through 26 feet of live steam, at 212 pounds pressure. From this they fall onto a steel, sawtooth cylinder, and pass under three soft rubber rolls, which crush the raisin and loosen the seeds. They then strike a corrugated steel roll, which throws out the seeds. The raisin passes on, is lifted from the cylinder by a steel rake and dropped into paraffine-paper-lined boxes, which are closed while the raisins are still hot from the steam sterilizing.

Steam is one of the commonest things in our kitchens. Until I went through the Food Products building I never realized how much it is used in the preparation of foods before they come to us. It sterilizes the raisins, cooks the oats before they are crushed into flakes for our breakfast oatmeal, puffs the rice, and cooks the wheat for the making of a well-known wheat biscuit.

A full sized unit of the factory which makes these biscuits is in operation near the raisin machine. In the preparation of this biscuit, after the wheat is screened and cleaned it is steam-cooked for 30 minutes, which softens the grain. It is then put into hoppers, which feed onto a corrugated steel cone, where the wheat is crushed into shreds. Each wheat berry makes a shred about 2 inches in length. These shreds fall from the cone into a narrow tray, which slowly moves back and forth on a carrier under the cone until it is full. Thirty-six layers of the shreds make the proper thickness. They are then cut into biscuit by steel knives, put on trays, and baked on revolving shelves in the oven. During all this process they are not touched by human hands. The moisture of the wheat and the heat of the baking combine to puff the biscuit to twice their former size.

Space forbids that I should describe the scores of exhibits in this enormous building devoted to the preparation of different foods, a task which always has been considered woman's work. I can only briefly mention the Japanese rice cakes—tiny bits of paste half an inch long and no thicker than paper. The smiling Oriental in charge drops them into boiling olive oil, and they puff into delicious-looking brown rolls 3 inches long. They look as toothsome as a home-made doughnut, but to your wild amazement, when you bite them there is nothing there.

I must say one word about the rose cakes, delicious cakes baked in the form of a rose, and as good as they are beautiful. And I am sure nobody leaves the exposition without speaking of the Scotch scones; everybody eats them who can reach them. They are baked by a Scotchman from Edinburg, who turns out more than 4,000 of them daily. They are buttered, spread with jam, and handed over the counter as fast as four girls can do it. And the counter is surrounded by a surging mob all day long.

As I went from booth to booth they gave me samples of the breads they had made with our American flour—the little, bland Chinese girl in her bright blue pajama costume, the smiling high-cheeked Russian peasant girl, the Hindoo in his gay turban, the swarthy, black-eyed Mexican—all of them eager to have me like their national foods. And I must say I did like most of it so well that I brought the recipes away with me, and pass them on to you:

Russian Forest

One pound flour, yolks of 3 eggs, 1 whole egg, ½ cup milk. Mix well and knead very thoroughly. Cut in pieces size of walnuts; roll very, very thin. Cut the center in strips, braid together and fry in deep fat. Drain, and sprinkle with powdered sugar.

Mexican Tamale Loaf

One pound veal, 1 onion, 2 cloves of garlic, 1 tablespoon chili powder, 1 can tomatoes (strained), 24 green olives (chopped). Boil the meat until very tender, take from the broth, cool and chop. Return to the broth, add salt to taste, add the onion and garlic chopped fine, then the tomatoes, garlic and chili powder. Let all come to the boiling point, then add enough yellow cornmeal to make as thick as mush, turn into molds and set aside to cool. The loaf may be served either cold or sliced and fried.

German Honey Cake

One cup honey, molasses or sirup; ½ cup sugar, 2 cups flour, 1 teaspoon cinnamon, 1 teaspoon cloves, 1 teaspoon ginger, 2 teaspoons baking powder. Beat honey and sugar 20 minutes, then add the spices, the baking powder, and lastly the flour. Pour into well-buttered baking sheets and bake 15 minutes in a moderate oven. Cover with chocolate icing and cut in squares.

Italian White Tagliarini

Three cups flour, ½ cup hot water, 2 eggs, 1 teaspoon salt. Mix and knead thoroughly, roll very thin as for noodles, and cut in any desired shape. Allow to dry 1 hour and cook in boiling water 10 minutes, drain, and serve with sauce.

Sauce for Tagliarini

One-half cup olive oil, 1 large pod garlic, 1 large carrot, 1 large can tomatoes, salt and pepper, 2 large onions, 5 stalks celery, 1 cup parsley, ½ pound hamburg steak, ⅛ teaspoon cloves, ½ cup butter. Heat the oil in an iron skillet or kettle, then add onions and garlic chopped fine. Cook until transparent but not brown, then add the rest of ingredients chopped fine. Cook slowly for 2 hours.

Croissonts (French Crescents)

Four cups flour, 1 cup warm water, 1 cake compressed yeast, ½ teaspoon salt, 1 cup butter. Sift and measure the flour into a bowl, add the yeast which has been dissolved in the water, then the salt. Mix and knead thoroughly. Let rise 2 or 3 hours, then roll out 1 inch thick and lay the butter on the center. Fold the dough over and roll out four times as for puff paste, then cut in pieces as for finger rolls, having the ends thinner than the middles. Form in crescent shape, brush with egg, and bake in a moderate oven.

Chinese Almond Cakes

Four cups flour, 1 cup lard, 1 ¼ cups sugar, 1 egg, ½ teaspoon baking powder. Mix and knead thoroughly. Take off pieces of dough the size of an English walnut, roll in a smooth round ball, then flatten about half. Make a depression on the top and place in it one almond. Place on pans, 2 inches apart, and bake a golden brown.

Unleavened Bread, or Matzas

From the earliest Bible times to the present, the Hebrew people have observed the feast of the Passover by eating unleavened bread. This bread is a hard cracker made from unfermented dough. The process of making is very simple. Mix flour and water to a very stiff dough. Roll this into a thin sheet, cut into round or square pieces, and bake in a hot oven.

Does it Pay to be Idle?

A stranger once went to a small inland town, in the Ozarks, to look over the country. As he left the little hotel, in the morning, for his day's wandering among the hills, he noticed several men sitting comfortably in the shade of the "gallery," gazing out into the street.

When the stranger returned late in the afternoon the "gallery" was still occupied by the same men, looking as though they had not stirred from their places since he left them there in the early morning.

This happened for three days and then as the stranger was coming in from his day's jaunt, in the evening he stopped and spoke to one of the men. "Say," he asked, "how do you fellows pass the time here all day? What do you do to amuse yourselves?"

The man emptied his mouth of its accumulation of tobacco juice and replied in a lazy drawl, "Oh we jest set and—think—and—sometimes—we—jest—set."

I have laughed many times over this story, which I know to be true, with never a thought, except for the humor of the tale, beyond the hackneyed ones on the value of wasted time; the vice of idleness.

We are told continually by everyone interested in our welfare or in "making the wheels go round," how to employ our spare moments to the best advantage, until, if we followed their advice, there would be no spare moments.

It is rank heresy, I know, to detract from these precepts, but lately I have been wondering whether perhaps it is not as great a fault to be too energetic as it is to be too idle.

Perhaps it would be better all round if we were to "jest set and think" a little more, or even sometimes "jest set."

Vices are simply overworked virtues, anyway. Economy and frugality are to be commended but carry them on in an increasing ratio and what do we find at the other end? A miser! If we overdo the using of spare moments we may find an invalid at the end, while perhaps if we allowed ourselves more idle time we would conserve our nervous strength and health to more than the value of the work we could accomplish by emulating at all times the busy little bee.

I know a woman, not very strong, who to the wonder of her friends, went through a time of extraordinary hard work without any ill effects.

I asked her for her secret and she told me that she was able to keep her health, under the strain, because she took 20 minutes, of each day, in which to absolutely relax both mind and body. She did not even "set and think." She lay at full length, every muscle and nerve relaxed and her mind as quiet as her body. This always relieved the strain and renewed her strength.

I spent a delightful day not long ago, visiting in a home where there are several children and the little mother not over strong. She is doing nothing to add to the family income; has no special work of her own to earn some pin money, but the way she has that little family organized would be a lesson in efficiency to many a business man. The training she is giving the children and the work she is doing in preparing them to meet the problems of life and become self-supporting, self-respecting citizens could not be paid for in money.

The children all help and the work for the day goes forward with no confusion. There is nothing left undone because one person thought another was to do it. There are no whines such as "I did that yesterday; let sister (or brother) do it this time." Each child has a particular part of the work to do. Each knows what their work is and that he is responsible for that work being done as it should be.

One of the girls does the upstairs work, another has the care of the parlor, dining room and library. The two smaller girls must keep their playthings in order and not leave their belongings scattered around the house. The mother does the cooking and washing the dishes. The places are changed from time to time that there may be no unfairness and that each may learn to do the different kinds of work. One boy keeps water in the house, milks the cow and keeps the motor car clean. Another boy brings in the wood and runs errands. Each receives for the work done a few cents a week and this is their spending money, to do with as they please. When it is spent there is no teasing for a few cents to spend on this or that. They know the amount of their income and plan and spend accordingly. In this way they are learning the value of money; to work for what they want instead of begging for it and to live within their income. If their work is not well done, a fine of a few cents is a better punishment than a scolding or a whipping, leaving both parties with their self-respect uninjured, while the child can see that the punishment fits the crime.

"*I* don't know what to do with Edith," said a mother to me. "I've no idea where she learned it, but she is a regular little liar. I can't depend on a thing she says."

Edith was a very bright, attractive child about three years old. Just then she started to go into another room. "Oh! Don't go in there!" her mother exclaimed. "It's dark in there, and there is a big dog behind the door." The child opened the door a crack, peeped around it, smiled a knowing smile and went on in. Evidently she knew her mother and that she "could not depend on a thing she said," that she was "a regular little —" Sounds ugly, doesn't it? Perhaps I would better not quote it at all, but where do you suppose Edith learned to be untruthful?

When I went to San Francisco last summer, I left The Man Of The Place and his hired man to "batch it." There was no woman relative near, no near neighbors with whom they could board and of course it was out of the question to hire a girl to stay with two lone men. I was sorry for them, but our only child lives in San Francisco and I had not seen her for four years. Besides, there was the fair, so I left them and went.

Now the man of the place says, "If any man thinks housekeeping is easy work and not all a woman ought to do, just let him roll up his sleeves and tackle the job."

More than any other business, that of farming depends upon the home and it is almost impossible for any farmer to succeed without the help of the house. In the country the home is still depended on to furnish bed and board and the comforts of life.

It is a good idea sometimes to think of the importance and dignity of our every-day duties. It keeps them from being so tiresome; besides others are apt to take us at our own valuation.

Ruralist Prize Recipes

Chocolate Custard Pie
Six eggs, 2 ⅔ cups sweet milk, 5 tablespoons grated chocolate, 1 ½ cups sugar. Mix the milk and chocolate together. Beat the yolks of eggs to a cream, add sugar and beat thoroughly, add the other ingredients and season with vanilla. Beat the whites of the eggs to a stiff froth, stir in 2 tablespoons white sugar, put on top of the pies and bake in one crust. This makes two pies. (E.M.K., Callao, Mo.)

Ginger Cookies
Boil together ½ cup of sugar, 1 pint molasses, 1 cup butter. When cool mix with 2 well beaten eggs, 1 tablespoon soda, 1 to 2 tablespoons ginger according to taste, and flour to roll. (Mrs. William T. Cross, Hattie, Mo.)

Join the "Don't Worry" Club

CONSERVATION OF A WOMAN'S STRENGTH IS TRUE PREPAREDNESS

"Eliminate—to thrust out." Did you never hear of the science of elimination? Didn't know there was such a science! Well, just try to eliminate, or thrust out, from your everyday life, the unnecessary, hindering things and if you do not decide that it takes a great deal of knowledge to do so successfully, then I will admit that it was my mistake.

The spring rush is almost upon us. The little chickens, the garden, the spring sewing and house-cleaning will be on our hands soon, and the worst of it is they will all come together, unless we have been very wise in our planning.

It almost makes one feel like the farmer's wife who called up the stairs to awaken the hired girl on a Monday morning. "Liza Jane," she called, "come hurry and get up and get the breakfast. This is wash day and here it is almost 6 o'clock and the washing not done yet. Tomorrow is ironing day and the ironing not touched, next day is churning day and not begun and here the week is half gone and nothing done yet."

You'd hardly believe it but it's true. And it's funny, of course, but one can just feel the worry and strain under which she was suffering. All without reason, too, as the greater part of our worry usually is.

It seems to me that the first thing that should be "thrust out" from our household arrangements is that same worry and feeling of hurry. I do not mean to eliminate haste, for sometimes, usually in fact, that is necessary, but there is a wide difference between haste and hurry. We may make haste with our hands and feet and still keep our minds unhurried. If our minds are cool and collected our "heads" will be able to "save our heels" a great deal.

An engineer friend once remarked of the housekeeping of a capable woman, "There is no lost motion there." She never worried over her work. She appeared to have no feeling of hurry. Her mind, calm and quiet, directed the work of her hands and there was no bungling, no fruitless running here and there. Every motion and every step counted so that there was "no lost motion."

Household help is so very hard to get especially on the farm, that, with the housekeeper, it has become a question of what to leave undone or cut out altogether from her scheme of things as well as how to do in an easier manner what must be done.

The Man of The Place loved good things to eat.[2] Does yet, for that matter, as, indeed, I think men of all other places do. Trying to make him think I was a wonder of a wife I gratified this appetite, until at last, when planning the dinner for a feast day, I discovered to my horror that there was nothing extra I could cook to mark the day as being distinct and better than any other day. Pies, the best I could make, were common, every-day affairs. Cakes, ditto. Puddings, preserves and jellies were ordinary things. Fried, roasted, broiled and boiled poultry of all kinds was no treat, we had so much of it as well as other kinds of meat raised on the farm. By canning and pickling and preserving all kinds of vegetables and fruits we had each and every kind the year around. In fact, we were surfeited with good things to eat all the time.

As I studied the subject it was impressed upon me, that in order to thoroly enjoy anything, one must feel the absence of it at times and I acted upon that theory. We have fresh fruit the year around: our apples bridging the gap from blackberries and plums in the summer to the first strawberries in the spring, and these fresh fruits are usually our desserts. Fresh fruits are better, more healthful, more economical, and so much less work to serve than pies, puddings and preserves. These things we have on our feast days, for Sunday treats and for company. They are relished so much more because they are something different.

I stopped canning vegetables altogether. There is enough variety in winter vegetables, if rightly used, and we enjoy the green garden truck all the more for having been without it for a few months. The family is just as well if not better satisfied under this treatment and a great deal of hard work is left out.

Some time ago the semi-annual house-cleaning was dropped from my program, very much to everyone's advantage. If a room needed cleaning out of season, I used to think "Oh well, it will soon be house-cleaning time" and let it wait until then. I found that I was becoming like the man who did "wish Saturday would come so that he could take a bath." Then I decided I would have no more house-cleaning in the accepted meaning of that word.

The first step in the new order of things was to dispense with carpets and use rugs instead. When a rug needs shaking and airing it gets it then, or as soon as possible, instead of waiting until house-cleaning time. If the windows need washing they are washed the first day I feel energetic enough. The house is gone over in this way a little at a time when it is needed and as suits my convenience and about all that is left of the bugaboo of house-cleaning is the putting up of the heater in the fall and taking it out in the spring.

Never do I have the house in a turmoil and myself exhausted as it used to be when I house-cleaned twice a year.

To be sure there are limits to the lessening of work. I could hardly go so far as a friend who said, "Why sweep? If I let it go today and tomorrow and the next day there will be just so much gained, for the floor will be just as clean when I do sweep, as it would be if I swept every day from now until then." Still after all there is something to be said from that viewpoint. The applied science of the elimination of work can best be studied by each housekeeper for herself, but believe me, it is well worth studying.

During the first years of his married life, a man of my acquaintance, used to complain bitterly to his wife, because she did not make enough slop in the kitchen to feed a hog. "At home," he said, "they always kept a couple of hogs and they did not cost a cent for there was always enough waste and slop from the kitchen to feed them." How ridiculous we all are at times! This man actually thought that something was wrong instead of being thankful that there was no waste from his kitchen. The young wife was grieved, but said she did not "like to cook well enough to cook things and throw them to the hogs, for the sake of cooking more." The food on her table was always good even if some of it was made over dishes, and after a time her husband realized that he had a treasure in the kitchen and that it was much cheaper to feed the hogs their proper food than to give them what had been prepared for human consumption.

There are so many little heedless ways in which a few cents are wasted here and a few more there. The total would be truly surprising if we should sum them up. I illustrated this to myself in an odd way lately. While looking over the pages of a catalog advertising articles from 2 cents to 10 cents the Man of The Place said, "There are a good many little tricks you'd like to have. Get what you want; they will only cost a few cents." So I made out a list of what I wanted, things I decided I could not get along without, as I found them, one by one, on those alluring pages. I was surprised when I added up the cost to find that it amounted to $5. I put the list away intending to go over it and cut out some things to make the total less. That was several months ago and I have not yet missed any of the things I would have ordered. I have decided to let the list wait until I do.

Matches are small things to economize in, but why throw away even a match when it is just as easy to save it? In using an oil stove with several burners, I found that full half or more of the expense for matches could be saved by using the same match more than once. It was just as easy to touch the end of a used match to the flame already burning as it was to strike a new one. The only trouble necessary was to have an extra match safe in which to drop the match the first time it was used. When lighting the next burner it was just as easy to take the match from there as from the first match safe. A small thing, if you please, but small things have such a way of counting up. Everyone has heard the old saying that "a woman can throw more out of the window with a teaspoon than a man can throw in the door with a shovel." Of course, that is an exaggeration. I'm sure it couldn't be done, anyway not if the man shoveled right hard!

We are told that in the struggle of the nations for existence, and in our own if it should be drawn into the vortex, a great deal depends upon the organization of the economic resources; that in the last analysis the strength of nations as of individuals rests upon the kitchens of the country.

If economy is so essential in war time why is it not a good thing in time of peace? If it so strengthens a nation in time of stress, would it not make a nation more powerful if practiced at other times? Things cannot be considered small that have so great an effect!

With worry, waste and unnecessary work eliminated from our households we would be in a state of "preparedness" to which no one could possibly have any objection. And the beauty of it is that such a state of preparedness in our home is good in war or peace, for both nations and individuals.

Do Not Waste Your Strength

"Clothes are much more sanitary if not ironed after washing," said a physician in an article, on fresh air and sunshine which I read the other day. Isn't that delightful news and especially so in hot weather?[3] I have not ironed knit underwear, stockings, sheets or towels for years but, altho I knew there was a very good reason for not doing so, I have always felt rather apologetic about it. Science is surely helping the housewife! Now instead of fearing that the neighbors will say I am lazy or a poor housekeeper, when they find out that I slight my ironing, I can say: "Oh no, I never do much ironing, except the outside clothes. We must not iron out the fresh air and sunshine, you know. It is much more healthful not, the doctors say." Seriously, there is something very refreshing about sheets and pillow slips just fresh from the line, after being washed and dried in the sun and air. Just try them that way and see if your sleep is not sweeter.

Our inability to see things that are right before our eyes, until they are pointed out to us, would be amusing if it were not at times so serious. We are coming, I think, to depend too much on being told and shown and taught instead of using our own eyes and brains and inventive faculties, which are likely to be just as good as any other person's.

I should like to know who designed our furniture as we use it today? It must have been a man. No woman, I am sure, at least no woman who has the care of a house, would ever have made it as it is. Perhaps, if some physician or some domestic science teacher would point out to us the unnecessary dirt and the extra work caused by the height of our furniture, we would insist on having it different. Otherwise it is quite likely we shall keep on in the same old way, breaking our backs and overworking tired muscles, or we shall become careless and let the dirt accumulate.

Most furniture, and especially that in the bedroom, where of all places cleanliness should be most observed, is just high enough from the floor to permit dust and dirt to gather underneath but not high enough to be cleaned easily. It is more than likely, also, not fit to back smoothly against the wall but to set out just far enough to make a another hiding place for dust. The only way to clean under and behind such articles is to move them bodily from their place, clean the wall and floor and then move them back. This should be done every few days. However, dragging heavy dressers and wardrobes from the their places and then putting them back again is hard work and it is a great deal worse than time wasted to do it.

Built-in furniture does away with a great deal of heavy work. A little built-in cupboard and a light dressing table may take the place of the heavy dresser. One does not have to clean under, behind, or on top of closets and wardrobes that reach smoothly from floor to ceiling, nor do sideboards and china closets built into the walls need to be moved when cleaning the dining room.

All the World is Queer

"All the world is queer, except thee and me," said the old Quaker to his wife, "and sometimes I think thee is a little queer."

The Man of The Place once bought me a patent churn. "Now," said he, "throw away that old dash churn. This churn will bring the butter in 3 minutes." It was very kind of him. He had thought the churn would please me and to lighten my work, but I looked upon it with a little suspicion. There was only one handle to turn and opposite was a place to attach the power from a small engine. We had no engine so the churning must needs be done with one hand, while the other steadied the churn and held it down. It was hard to do, but the butter did come quickly and I would have used it anyway because the Man of The Place had been so kind.

The tin paddles which worked the cream were sharp on the edges and they were attached to the shaft by a screw which was supposed to be loosened to remove the paddles for washing, but I could never loosen it and usually cut my hands on the sharp tin. However, I used the new churn, one hand holding it down to the floor with grim resolution, while the other turned the handle with the strength of despair when the cream thickened. Finally it seemed that I could use it no longer. "I wish you would bring in my old dash churn," I said to the Man of The Place. "I believe it is easier to use than this after all."

"Oh!" said he: "you can churn in 3 minutes with this and the old one takes half a day. Put one end of a board on the churn and the other on a chair and sit on the board, then you can hold the churn down easily!" And so, when I churned I sat on the board in the correct mode for horseback riding and tho the churn bucked some I managed to hold my seat. "I wish," said I to the Man of The Place, "you would bring my old dash churn." (It was where I could not get it.) "I cut my hands on these paddles every time I wash them."

"Oh, pshaw!" said he, "you can churn with this churn in 3 minutes—"

One day when the churn had been particularly annoying and had cut my hand badly, I took the mechanism of the churn, handle, shaft, wheels and paddles all attached, to the side door which is quite high from the ground and threw it as far as I could. It struck on the handle, rebounded, landed on the paddles, crumpled and lay still and I went out and kicked it before I picked it up. The handle was broken off, the shaft was bent and the paddles were a wreck.

"I wish," I remarked casually to the Man of The Place, "that you would bring my old dash churn. I want to churn this morning."

"Oh, use the churn you have," said he. "You can churn in 3 minutes with it. What's the use to spend half a day"—

"I can't," I interrupted. "It's broken."

"Why, how did that happen?" he asked.

"I dropped it—just as far as I could," I answered in a small voice and he replied regretfully, "I wish I had known that you did not want to use it. I would like to have the wheels and shaft, but they're ruined now."

This is not intended as a condemnation of patent churns—there are good ones—but as a reminder that being new and patented is no proof that such a thing is better, even tho some smooth tongued agent has persuaded us that it will save time.

Also, as the old Quaker remarked to his wife, "Sometimes I think thee is a little queer."

Thanksgiving Time

Here is the first telling of the story (it occurs again at the end of chapter 26 in *By the Shores of Silver Lake*) of how Laura and Mary quarreled over whether there should be sage in the stuffing for the Thanksgiving goose.

As Thanksgiving day draws near again, I am reminded of an occurrence of my childhood. To tell the truth, it is a yearly habit of mine to think about this time and to smile at it once more.

We were living on the frontier in South Dakota then. There's no more frontier within the boundaries of the United States, more's the pity, but then we were ahead of the railroad in a new unsettled country. Our nearest and only neighbor was 12 miles away and the store was 40 miles distant.

Father had laid in a supply of provisions for the winter and among them were salt meats, but for fresh meat we depended on father's gun and the antelope which fed, in herds, across the prairie. So we were quite excited, one day near Thanksgiving, when father hurried into the house for his gun and then away again to try for a shot at a belated flock of wild geese hurrying south.

We would have roast goose for Thanksgiving dinner! "Roast goose and dressing seasoned with sage," said sister Mary. "No, not sage! I don't like sage and we won't have it in the dressing," I exclaimed. Then we quarreled, sister Mary and I, she insisting that there should be sage in the dressing and I declaring there should not be sage in the dressing, until father returned,—without the goose! I remember saying in a meek voice to sister Mary, "I wish I had let you have the sage," and to this day when I think of it I feel again just as I felt then and realize how thankful I would have been for roast goose and dressing with sage seasoning—with or without any seasoning—I could even have gotten along without the dressing. Just plain goose roasted would have been plenty good enough.

This little happening has helped me to be properly thankful even tho at times the seasoning of my blessings has not been such as I would have chosen.

"I suppose I should be thankful for what we have, but I can't feel very thankful when I have to pay $2.60 for a little flour and the price still going up," writes a friend, and in the same letter she says, "we are in our usual health." The family are so used to good health that it is not even taken into consideration as a cause of thanksgiving. We are so inclined to take for granted the blessings we possess and to look for something peculiar, some special good luck for which to be thankful.

I read a Thanksgiving story, the other day, in which a woman sent her little boy out to walk around the block and look for something for which to be thankful.

One would think that the fact of his being able to walk around the block and that he had a mother to send him would have been sufficient cause for thankfulness. We are nearly all afflicted with mental farsightedness and so easily overlook the thing which is obvious and near. There are our hands and feet,—whoever thinks of giving thanks for them, until indeed they, or the use of them, are lost. We usually accept them as a matter of course, without a thought, but a year of being crippled has taught me the value of my feet and two perfectly good feet are now among my dearest possessions. Why! There is a greater occasion for thankfulness just in the unimpaired possession of one of the five senses than there would be if some one left us a fortune. Indeed, how could the value of one be reckoned? When we have all five in good working condition we surely need not make a search for anything else in order to feel that we should give thanks to Whom thanks are due.

I once remarked how happy and cheerful a new acquaintance seemed always to be and the young man to whom I spoke replied, "Oh he's just glad that he is alive." Upon inquiry, I learned that several years before this man had been seriously ill, that there had been no hope of his living, but to everyone's surprise he had made a complete recovery and since then he had always been remarkably happy and cheerful.

So if for nothing else, let's "Just be glad that we are alive" and be doubly thankful if like the Scotch poet [Robert Burns], we have a good appetite and the means to gratify it.

> Some hae meat that canna eat
> And some want meat that lack it,
> But I hae meat and I can eat,
> And sae the Lord be thanket.

A Centerpiece for the Thanksgiving Dinner

(PRIZE LETTER, NOVEMBER 16, 1912)

To the Missouri *Ruralist*:

Each year the Thanksgiving dinner becomes more and more a family dinner, with none of the formality or elaboration of the "company" dinner. To be typical of our first Thanksgiving, it must be of harvest foods.

The decorations of the table should be as suggestive of autumn and of the harvest as the dinner itself. Vegetables, fruits and autumn leaves are as decorative as flowers and are far more suitable.

A golden "horn of plenty" may be made from a large crook-neck squash. Cut the end off it at the widest part and scoop out the inside (use in center of table), fill with fruits and place on bed of pine-sprays or fern fronds. Or if preferred a pumpkin may be used instead, and, filled with fruit and nuts, decorated with autumn leaves and bittersweet berries makes a pretty centerpiece.

—Lovie M. Tedford, Olin, Ia.

Before Santa Came

Christmas was always a genuinely special time for Laura, as her account here of the difference between the pagan and Christian forms of the solstice festival makes clear. Laura's most touching account of Christmas is perhaps in chapter 19 of *Little House on the Prairie,* "Mr. Edwards Meets Santa Claus." There Laura tells how Mr. Edwards, "the Tennessee wildcat," struggles through the night and wades a swollen river to bring Laura and Mary the gifts that Santa has given him to deliver. This piece is Laura's contribution to "Talking it over with Farm Folk," 'By Missouri Farmers.'

Hundreds of years ago when our pagan ancestors lived in the great forests of Europe and worshiped the sun, they celebrated Christmas in a somewhat different fashion than we do today.

The sun, they thought, was the giver of all good. He warmed and lighted the earth. He caused the grass to grow for their flocks and herds to eat and the fruits and rains for their own food, but every year after harvest time he became angry with them and started to go away, withdrawing his warmth and light farther and still farther from them. The days when he showed them his face became shorter and shorter and the periods of darkness ever longer. The farther away he went the colder it grew. The waters turned to ice and snow fell in place of the gentle summer showers.

If their god indeed left them as he seemed to be doing, if he would not become reconciled to them, they must all perish, for nothing would grow upon which they could live and if they did not freeze they would die of hunger. Their priests' prayers availed nothing and something must be done to make the sun god smile upon them once more. The priests demanded a human sacrifice, the sacrifice of a child!

What is now Christmas eve was the night chosen for the ceremony. On that night the door of every hut in the village must be left unfastened that the priests might enter and take the child. No one knew which house would be entered nor what child taken to be sacrificed on the altar of the Sun God.

Perhaps the priests knew that the shortest day of the year had arrived and that the sun would start on its return journey at this time. They may have taken advantage of this knowledge to gain greater control over the people, but it may be that the selection of the right day at first was purely accidental and they believed, with the people, that the Sun God was pleased by the sacrifice. It was, to them, proof of this that he immediately started to return and smiled upon them for another season.

Do you suppose the children knew and listened in terror for footsteps on Christmas eve? The fathers and mothers must have harkened for the slightest noise and waited in agony, not knowing whether their house would be passed by or whether the priests would enter stealthily and bear away one of their children or perhaps their only child. How happy they must have been when the teachers of Christianity came and told them it was all unnecessary. It is no wonder they celebrated the birth of Christ on the date of that awful night of sacrifice, which was now robbed of its terror, nor that they made it a children's festival.

Instead of the stealthy steps of cruel men, there came now, on Christmas eve, a jolly saint with reindeer and bells, bringing gifts. This new spirit of love and peace and safety that was abroad in the land did not require that the doors be left unbarred. He could come thru locked doors or down the chimney and be everywhere at once on Christmas night, for a spirit can do such things. No wonder the people laughed and danced and rang the joy bells on Christmas day and the celebration with its joy and thankfulness has come on down the years to us. Without all that Christmas means, we might still be dreading the day in the old terrible way instead of listening for the sleigh bells of Santa Claus.

The Christmas Turkey

(PRIZE RECIPE, DECEMBER 1912)

To the Missouri *Ruralist*:

Dress a nice young turkey, weighing from 10 to 12 pounds; the day before Christmas, salt and put away till morning.

The Stuffing—Take 2 pounds of hulled chestnuts, cook with the giblets until tender, mash the chestnuts then mix with 7 cups of bread crumbs, 2 cups of good rich cream, 2 cups of hot water, 1 egg well beaten, season with salt, pepper and sage.

To Roast Turkey—Rub its entire surface with butter until creamy, dredge with flour, place the bird breast downward in roasting pan to retain a rich juicy flavor. Place in hot oven and when flour begins to brown reduce heat. Add 3 cups of boiling water, baste every 15 minutes with a lump of butter melted in a cup of hot water. From 3 to 4 hours will be required to roast the bird. Before removing from oven turn on back to brown the breast. When done place on platter, garnish with cranberries and squares of dressing.

The Gravy—Place the pan the bird was cooked in on top of stove, add 4 cups of stock in which the giblets were cooked, add the chopped giblets, ¾ cup of good rich cream, about 6 spoonsful flour well blended in water before adding, to thicken. Stir well, season with salt and pepper and let boil.

—Mrs. Jesse Parkes, High Point, Mo.

To Buy or Not to Buy

I have been very much impressed by a sentence I read in an advertisement of farm machinery and here it is for you to think about. "The minute we need a thing, we begin paying for it whether we buy it or not."

That is true of farm machinery on the face of it. If a farm tool is actually needed it will, without question, have to be bought in time and the farmer begins paying for it at once in loss of time or waste or damaging result from not having it. He might even, if buying was put off long enough, pay the whole price of the machine and still not have it.

A dentist once said to me, "I don't care whether people come to me when they should, or put off coming as long as they possibly can. I know they'll come in time and the longer they put it off the bigger my bill will be when they do come." We begin to pay the dentist when our teeth first need attention whether they have that attention or not.

"I can't afford to build a machine shed this year," said Farmer Jones and so his machinery stood out in the weather to rot and rust. The next year he had to spend so much for repairs and new machines that he was less able than before to build the shed. He is paying for that protection for his machinery but he may never have it.

We think we cannot afford to give the children the proper schooling, "besides, their help is needed on the farm," we say. We shall pay for that education which we do not give them. Oh! We shall pay for it! When we see our children inefficient and handicapped, perhaps thru life, for the lack of the knowledge they should have gained in their youth, we shall pay in our hurt pride and our regret that we did not give them a fair chance, if in no other way, tho quite likely we shall pay in money too. The children, more's the pity, must pay also.

Mr. Colton's work kept him outdoors in all kinds of weather and one autumn he did not buy the warm clothing he needed. He said he could not afford to do so and would make the old overcoat last thru. The old coat outlasted him for he took a chill from exposure and died of pneumonia. So he paid with his life for a coat he never had and his widow paid the bills which amounted to a great deal more than the cost of an overcoat.

Instances multiply when one looks for them. We certainly do begin paying for a thing when we actually need it whether we buy it or not, but this is no plea for careless buying as it is just as great a mistake to buy what we do not need as it is not to buy what we should. In the one case we pay before and in the other we usually keep paying after the real purchase. One thing always leads to another or even to two or three and it requires good business judgment to buy the right thing at the right time.

"Thoughts are Things"

As someone has said, "thoughts are things," and the atmosphere of every home depends on the kind of thoughts each member of that home is thinking.

I spent an afternoon a short time ago with a friend in her new home. The house was beautiful and well furnished with new furniture but it seemed bare and empty to me. I wondered why this was until I remembered my experience with my new house. I could not make the living room seem homelike. I would move the chairs here and there and change the pictures on the wall, but something was lacking. Nothing seemed to change the feeling of coldness and vacancy that displeased me whenever I entered the room.

Then, as I stood in the middle of the room one day wondering what I could possibly do to improve it, it came to me that all that was needed was someone to live in it and furnish it with the everyday, pleasant thoughts of friendship and cheerfulness and hospitality.

We all know there is a spirit in every home, a sort of composite spirit composed of the thoughts and feelings of the members of the family as a composite photograph is formed of the features of different individuals. This spirit meets us at the door as we enter the home. Sometimes it is a friendly, hospitable spirit and sometimes it is cold and forbidding.

If the members of a home are ill-tempered and quarrelsome, how quickly you feel it when you enter the house. You may not know just what is wrong but you wish to make your visit short. If they are kindly, generous, good-tempered people you will have a feeling of warmth and welcome that will make you wish to stay. Sometimes you feel that you must be very prim and dignified and at another place you feel a rollicking good humor and a readiness to laugh and be merry. Poverty or riches, old style housekeeping or modern conveniences do not affect you feelings. It is the characters and personalities of the persons who live there.

Each individual has a share in making this atmosphere of the home what it is, but the mother can mold it more to her wish. I read a piece of poetry several years ago supposed to be a man speaking of his wife and this was the refrain of the little story:

> "I love my wife because she laughs,
> Because she laughs and doesn't care."

I'm sure that it would have been a delightful home to visit, for a good laugh overcomes more difficulties and dissipates more dark clouds than any other one thing. And this woman was the embodied spirit of cheerfulness and good temper.

Let's be cheerful! We have no more right to steal the brightness out of the day for own family than we have to steal the purse of a stranger. Let us be as careful that our homes are furnished with pleasant and happy thoughts as we are that the rugs are the right color and texture and the furniture comfortable and beautiful!

What We Do for Christmas

FIRST-PRIZE LETTER FROM: "MISSOURI BOYS AND GIRLS
TELL HOW TO ENTERTAIN NEIGHBORS AND
RELATIVES IN HOLIDAY TIME"

What could be more fun on Christmas Eve than a neighborhood party to which you invite all of your neighbors and friends? A Christmas tree should be the chief attraction of such an affair. Request each guest to bring a present to put on the tree. The tree selected should be large and well shaped. Strings of popcorn, paper chains, silver stars and tinsel will make attractive but inexpensive decorations. Each family should provide some ornament so as to make the tree as pretty as possible.

As the guests arrive, let someone previously appointed for this purpose receive the gifts and tie them on the tree. Then things will go smoothly and all will be in readiness at the proper time. The tree should be placed in one room and the guests ushered into another. When everything is ready the hostess should lead the guests into the adjoining room and the tree should be displayed.

After the children get over the excitement of this pretty sight, commence the program which has previously been arranged. This should include Christmas songs, piano solos, recitations and Christmas readings. A one-act play would also provide lots of amusement. The last number should be a Christmas song. While singing the final stanza have someone dressed as Santa Claus appear and let him deliver the presents.

After the presents have been distributed and opened, serve refreshments such as cake, sweet cider, candy and fruit. Then if not too late a few games may be played.

—Frances McKinzie, New Franklin, Mo.

Let's Visit Mrs. Wilder

Seven years after publishing Laura's first article, John Francis Case, the *Ruralist*'s editor, wrote this tribute to her. He describes Laura as "a writer and state leader."

Missouri farm folks need little introduction before getting acquainted with Mrs. A.J. Wilder of Rocky Ridge Farm. During the years that she has been associated with this paper—a greater number of years than any other person on the editorial staff— she has taken strong hold upon the esteem and affections of our great family. Mrs. Wilder has lived her life upon a farm. She knows farm folks and their problems as few women who write know them. And having sympathy with the folks whom she serves she writes well.

"Mrs. Wilder is a woman of delightful personality," a neighbor tells me, "and she is a combination of energy and determination. She always is cheery, looking on the bright side. She is her husband's partner in every sense and is fully capable of managing the farm. No woman can make you feel more at home than can Mrs. Wilder, and yet, when the occasion demands, she can be dignity personified. Mrs. Wilder has held high rank in the Eastern Star. The time when a Farm Loan association was formed at Mansfield she was made secretary-treasurer. When her report was sent to the Land Bank officials they told her the papers were perfect and the best sent in." As a final tribute Mrs. Wilder's friends said this: "She gets eggs in the winter when none of her neighbors gets them."

Born in Wisconsin

"I was born in a log house within 4 miles of the legend haunted Lake Pippin [Pepin] in Wisconsin," Mrs. Wilder wrote when I asked for information "about" her. "I remember seeing deer that my father had killed, hanging in the trees about our forest home. When I was four years old we traveled to the Indian Territory, Fort Scott, Kan., being our nearest town. My childish memories hold the sound of the war whoop and I see pictures of painted Indians."

Looking at the picture of Mrs. Wilder, which was recently taken, we find it difficult to believe that she is old enough to be the pioneer described. But having confided her age to the editor (not for publication)[4] we must be convinced that it is true. Surely Mrs. Wilder, who is the mother of Rose Wilder Lane, talented author and writer, has found the fountain of youth in the Ozark hills. We may well believe she has a "cheerful disposition" as her friend asserts.

"I was a regular little tomboy," Mrs. Wilder confesses, "and it was fun to walk the 2 miles to school." The folks were living in Minnesota then but it was not long until Father Ingalls, who seems to have had a penchant for moving about, had located in Dakota. It was at DeSmet, South Dakota, that Laura Ingalls, then 18 years old, married A.J. Wilder, a farmer boy. "Our daughter, Rose Wilder Lane, was born on the farm," Mrs. Wilder informs us, "and it was there I learned to do all kinds of farm work with machinery. I have ridden the binder, driving six horses. And I could ride. I do not wish to appear conceited, but I broke my own ponies to ride. Of course they were not bad but they were bronchos." Mrs. Wilder had the spirit that brought success to the pioneers.

Mr. Wilder's health failed and the Wilders went to Florida. "I was something of a curiosity, being the only 'Yankee girl' the inhabitants had ever seen," Mrs. Wilder relates. The low altitude did not agree with Mrs. Wilder tho and she became ill. It was then[5] that they came to Rocky Ridge Farm, near Mansfield, Wright county, and there they have lived for 25 years. Only 40 acres was purchased and the land was all timber except a 4 acre worn-out field. "Illness and traveling expenses had taken all our surplus cash and we lacked $150 of paying for the 40 acres," Mrs. Wilder writes. "Mr. Wilder was unable to do a full day's work. The garden, my hens and the wood I helped saw and which we sold in town took us thru the first year. It was then I became an expert at the end of a crosscut saw and I still can 'make a hand' in an emergency. Mr. Wilder says he would rather have me help than any man he ever sawed with. And, believe me, I learned how to take care of hens and make them lay."

Intelligent industry brings its own rewards. Mr. and Mrs. Wilder not only paid for the 40 acres but they have added 60 acres more, stocked the farm to capacity and improved it and built a beautiful modern home. "Everything sold by the Wilders brings a good price," their neighbor tells me, "because it is standard goods. It was by following strict business methods that they were enabled to build their beautiful home. Most of the material used was found on the farm. Fortunate indeed are those who are entertained at Rocky Ridge."

One may wonder that so busy a person as Mrs. Wilder can find time to write. "I always have been a busy person," she says, "doing my own housework, helping the Man of the Place when help could not be obtained, but I love to work. And it is a pleasure to write for the Missouri *Ruralist*. And Oh I do just love to play! The days never have been long enough to do the things I would like to do. Every year has held more of interest than the year before." Folks who possess that kind of spirit get a lot of joy out of life as they travel the long road.

Joined the Family in 1911

Mrs. Wilder has held numerous important offices and her stories about farm life and farm folk have appeared in the best farm papers.[6] Her first article printed in the Missouri *Ruralist* appeared in February, 1911. It was a copy of an address prepared for Farmers' Week. So for seven years she has been talking to Missouri women thru these columns; talk that always has carried inspiration and incentive for worth while work.

Reading Mrs. Wilder's contributions most folks doubtless have decided that she is a college graduate. But, "my education has been what a girl would get on the frontier," she informs us. "I never graduated from anything and only attended high school two terms." Folks who know Mrs. Wilder tho, know that she is a cultured, well-educated gentlewoman. Combined with inherent ability, unceasing study of books has provided the necessary education and greater things have been learned from the study of life itself.

As has been asserted before, Mrs. Wilder writes well for farm folks because she knows them. The Wilders can be found ready to enter wholeheartedly into any movement for community betterment and the home folks are proud of the reputation that Mrs. Wilder has established. They know that she has won recognition as a writer and state leader because of ability alone.

Notes for "Making a Home"

1. Liberty Hyde Bailey, 1858–1954, was professor of horticulture (1888–1903) and director of the Agricultural Research Station (1903–13) at Cornell University, New York. His botanical scholarship was in North American sedges, blackberries, raspberries, New World palms, and the systematics of cultivated plants (his most famous work, written with Ethel Zoe Bailey, being *Hortus*, a comprehensive dictionary of plants cultivated in the United States and Canada). He also wrote extensively on rural problems and education.

2. Laura's second book, *Farmer Boy*, deals at some length with young Almanzo's extraordinary appetite. Chapters 8, "Sunday," and 26, "Christmas," contain accounts of the makings of a champion eater—and examples of Laura's tasty way of describing food.

3. Laura was writing in the days when most irons still had to be heated on a hot stove.

4. When the article was published Laura was twelve days past her fifty-first birthday.

5. The story here is abbreviated In 1890, after a series of disasters (crop failures, the death of their second child, the burning down of their home, and the diphtheria that left Almanzo lame for the rest of his life), Laura, Rose, and Almanzo left De Smet for Spring Valley, Minnesota, where they spent a year on the farm belonging to Almanzo's parents.

Laura's cousin Peter had settled in the Florida Panhandle, and thinking that the warm climate might be good for Almanzo's health, the Wilders decided to try their luck there. They were greeted with such hostility and suspicion, however, that Laura began to carry a revolver in her skirt pocket, and in August 1891, after less than a year in Florida, the Wilders returned to De Smet. There they rented a house in town. Almanzo worked at carpentry and odd jobs, while Laura turned her hand to dressmaking for $1 an hour. At length the Wilders saw advertisements put out by Missouri land developers, and talked with a neighbor who had traveled to the Ozarks and come back with glowing stories of the "Land of the Big Red Apple."

In the summer of 1894, the Wilders—with Laura still carrying her little silver revolver—set out by wagon on their journey to Mansfield and Rocky Ridge Farm.

6. Laura's work also appeared in the St. Louis *Star Farmer*, the St. Louis *Post Dispatch*, and the Kansas City *Star*.

The Ways of the World

Life is an Adventure

VOYAGES OF DISCOVERY CAN BE MADE IN YOUR ROCKING CHAIR

In this article Laura describes the excitement of visiting San Francisco and observing its ethnically diverse society. At times her language may be rather shocking for today's readers, but it reflects the speech of her period, not any personal prejudice. Laura had never previously seen much of Asian or African Americans, and the sight of them in San Francisco was wonderful to her, and not a cause for hostility. In *Little House in the Big Woods* she describes how her very first visit to a town, Pepin, was so exciting that she "could scarcely breathe." San Francisco and the Great Exposition had much the same effect on her in 1915.

Throughout her writings there is evidence that Laura was unusually open to people of other races. In *Little House on the Prairie*, she describes how she can hardly wait to see an Indian baby, a "papoose," and in general she is far less fearful of the Indians than her mother or sister Mary. When she describes the Indian leader Soldat du Chêne (who probably saved the Ingalls' lives), what strikes her most is the man's dignity. Her diary of the journey from South Dakota to the Ozarks (published as *On the Way Home*) also records her respect for and sympathy with the Indians. At the Bluffs of the James River, in South Dakota, she notes that if she had been an Indian she "would have scalped more white folks before I ever would have left it," and in her *Ruralist* article "When is a Settler an Old Settler," she recognizes the precedence of the American Indians in the settled land.

Perhaps the best statement of Laura's attitude to people of other races is to be found in "Our Fair and Other Things," a *Ruralist* article written in November 1916, where she writes "It is not alone 'one touch of nature' which 'makes the whole world kin,' but every emotion which writes itself on the human countenance creates a family likeness, with others of its kind, even between people of different races."

As I was passing through the Missouri building at the exposition last summer, I heard a scrap of conversation between two women. Said the first woman, "How do you like San Francisco?" The other replied, "I don't like San Francisco at all! Everywhere I go there is a Chinaman on one side, a Jap on the other and a nigger behind."

These women were missing a great deal, for the foreign life of San Francisco is very interesting and the strange vari-colored peoples on the streets give a touch of color and picturesqueness that adds much to the charm of the city. A morning's walk from the top of Russian Hill, where I lived when there, would lead me to "Little Italy" where one hears Italian spoken on all sides; where the people are black-eyed and handsome with a foreign beauty and where, I am sure, the children are the most beautiful in the world.

From here I passed daily into "Chinatown" where the quaint babies look exactly like Chinese dolls and the older people look as if they had stepped out of a Chinese picture. The women in their comfortable loose garments made of black or soft colored silks, with their shiny, smoothly combed black hair full of bright ornaments, were, some of them, very pretty. Only the older men seemed to be wearing the Chinese dress. The younger men were dressed like any American business man. It is a curious fact that the second generation of Chinese born in San Francisco are much larger than their parents and look a great deal like our own people, while the third generation can scarcely be distinguished from Americans. And oh the shops of Chinatown! I do not understand how any woman could resist their fascination. Such quaint and wonderful jewelry, such wonderful pieces of carved ivory, such fine pottery, and silks and embroideries as one finds there!

Wandering on from Chinatown I would soon be at Market street, which is the main business street of San Francisco, and everywhere, as the women in the Missouri building had said, there was "a Chinaman on one side, a Jap on the other, and a nigger behind."

It gives a stay-at-home Middle Westerner something of a shock to meet a group of turbaned Hindoos on the street, or a Samoan, a Filipino or even a Mexican. People in happier times spent hundreds of dollars and months of time in traveling to see these foreign people and their manner of living. It is all to be seen, on a smaller scale, in this city of our own country.

Walking on the Zone one day at the fair, Daughter and I noticed ahead of us five sailormen. They were walking along discussing which one of the attractions they should visit. They were evidently on shore for a frolic. Tired of "rocking in the cradle of the deep," they were going to enjoy something different on shore. Should they see the wonderful educated horse? "No!" Who cares anything about an old horse?" Should they see Creation, the marvelous electrical display? "No! Not that! We're here for a good time, aren't we?" Perhaps by now you suspect that Daughter and I had become so interested we determined to know which of the attractions they decided was worth while. We followed with the crowd at their heels. The sailors passed the places of amusement one after another until they came to a mimic river, with a wharf and row boats, oars and all. Immediately they made a rush for the wharf and the last we saw of them they were tumbling hilariously into one of the boats, for a good old row on the pleasant familiar water.

Do you know, they reminded me someway, of the women in the Missouri building who did not like San Francisco.

A friend of mine tried to sympathize with a woman for being "tied down" to a farm, with no opportunity to travel or study; and with none of the advantages of town or city life. To her surprise she found that her sympathy was not needed. "My body may be tied here," her friend said, "but my mind is free. Books and papers are cheap and what I cannot buy I can borrow. I have traveled all over the world."

The daughter of this woman was raised with a varied assortment of these same books and papers, pictures and magazines. When later she traveled over the United States, becoming familiar with the larger cities as well as the country, from Canada to the Gulf and from San Francisco to New York City, she said there was a great disappointment to her in traveling. She seemed to have seen it all before and thus had no "thrills" from viewing strange things. "I have read about foreign countries just as much" she said "and don't suppose I'll find anything in the world that will be entirely new to me." Which shows that a very good travel education can be had from books and papers and also proves once more the old saying that, "As the twig is bent the tree inclines."

Over at a neighbor's, the other day, I learned something new, as by the way quite often happens. She has little soft home-made mattresses as thick as a good comfort to lay over the top of the large mattresses on her beds. Over these small mattresses she slips a cover as one does on a pillow. They are easily removed for washings and protect the mattress from soil, making it a simple matter to keep the beds clean and sweet.

This neighbor also makes her sheets last twice as long, by a little trick she has. When the sheets begin to wear thin in the middle she tears them down the center and sews the outsides together. Then she hems the outer edges down the sides. This throws the thin part to the outside and the center, where the wear comes, is as good as new. Of course the sheet has a seam down the middle, but it is not so very many years ago that all our sheets were that way, before we had sheeting and pillow tubing.

It is no use trying! I seem unable today to get away from the idea of travel, perhaps because I read the "National Geographic Magazine" last night. A sentence in one of the articles keeps recurring to me and I am going to quote it to you for you may not have noticed it. "It is not a figure of speech to say that every American has it in his heart that he is in a small sense a discoverer; that he is joining in the revelation to the world of something that it was not before aware of and of which it may some day make use."

We have the right, you know, to take a thought and appropriate it to our own uses, and so I have been turning this one over and over in my mind with all sorts of strange ramifications. The greater number of us cannot be discoverers of the kind referred to in the article quoted, for like the woman before mentioned, our bodies are tied more or less securely to our home habitat, but I am sure we are discoverers at heart. Life is often called a journey, "the journey of life." Usually when referred to in these terms it is also understood that it is "a weary pilgrimage." Why not call it a voyage of discovery and take it in the spirit of happy adventure?

Adventurers and travelers worthy the name always make nothing of the difficulties they meet; nor are they so intent on the goal that they do not make discoveries on the way. Has anyone ever said to you, as a warning, "No man knoweth what a day may bring forth?" I have heard it often and it is always quoted with a melancholy droop at the corners of the mouth. But why! Suppose we do not know what will happen tomorrow. May it not just as well be a happy surprise as something unpleasant? To me it is a joy that "no man knoweth what a day may bring forth" and that life is a journey from one discovery to another. It makes of every day a real adventure; and if things are not to my liking today, why, "There's a whole day tomorrer that ain't teched yet," as the old darkey said, "No man knoweth" what the day will be like. It is absolutely undiscovered country. I'll just travel along and find out for myself. Did you ever take a little trip anywhere with your conscience easy about things at home, your mind free from worry; and with all care cast aside and eyes wide open, give yourself to the joy of every passing incident; looking for interesting things which happen every moment? If you have, you will understand. If not, you should try it and you will be surprised how much of adventure can enter into ordinary things.

Look for Fairies Now

THE "LITTLE PEOPLE" STILL APPEAR TO THOSE WITH SEEING EYES

Laura's plea here for a more metaphysical view of the fairy realm prefigures the story in chapter 12 of *On the Banks of Plum Creek,* "The Christmas Horses." There Ma tells the girls that Santa Claus is everywhere, all the time, and that "Whenever anyone was unselfish, that was Santa Claus." And in chapter 16 of *The Long Winter,* "Fair Weather," Laura explains to Carrie how it is that the bad weather won't stop Santa Claus's visit. The reason, she says, is that "Santa Claus can come anywhere."

Have you seen any fairies lately? I asked the question of a little girl not long ago. "Huh! There's no such things as fairies," she replied. Some way the answer hurt me and I have been vaguely disquieted when I have thought of it ever since. By the way, have you seen any fairies lately? Please do not answer as the little girl did, for I'm sure there are fairies and that you at least have seen their work.

In the long, long ago days when the farmers gathered their crops they always left a part of whatever crop they were harvesting in or on the ground for the use of the "Little People." This was only fair for the "Little People" worked hard in the ground to help the farmer grow his crops and if a share were not left for them they became angry and the crops would not be good the next year. You may laugh at this as an old superstition but I leave it to you if it has not been proved true that where the "Little People" of the soil are not fed the crops are poor. We call them different names now, nitrogen and humus and all the rest of it, but I always have preferred to think of them as fairy folk who must be treated right. Our agricultural schools and farm papers spend much time and energy telling us to put back into the soil the elements of which we rob it. Only another way of saying, "Don't rob the 'Little People'; feed them!"

Dryads used to live in the trees you know, beautiful, fairy creatures who now and then were glimpsed beside the tree into which they vanished. There have been long years during which we have heard nothing of them, but now scientists have discovered that leaves of trees have eyes, actual eyes that mirror surrounding objects. Of what use are eyes to a tree, I wonder? Would it not be fine if the men of science gave us back all our fairies under other names?

There is the old myth of Santa Claus! What child in these deadly, matter-of-fact times believes in Santa Claus; yet who can deny that at Christmas time there is a spirit, bringing gifts, abroad in the world; who can come down the chimney, or through the keyhole for that matter, and travel in the same night from the north pole to the south? Why not let the children believe in Santa Claus? Later they will understand that it is only a beautiful imagery. It is surely no harm to idealize things and make them more real by investing them with personalities and it might do away with some of the sordid estimating of the price of gifts, which children learn so surprisingly young.

I have a feeling that childhood has been robbed of a great deal of its joys by taking away its belief in wonderful, mystic things, in fairies and all their kin. It is not surprising that when children are grown they have so little idealism or imagination nor that so many of them are like the infidel who asserted that he would not believe anything he could not see. It was a good retort the Quaker made, "Friend! Does thee believe thee has any brains?"

It is astonishing what an effect a child's early training has upon its whole life. When one reflects upon the subject one is inclined to agree with the noted clergyman who said, "Give me the child for the first seven years of his life and you may have him all the rest of the time." What a wonderful power mothers have in the their hands! They shape the lives of the children today, thru¹ them the lives of the men and women of tomorrow, and thru them the nations and the world.

I see by the papers that one of the suffrage leaders of the state will tour the Ozarks this spring in the interest of woman suffrage, bringing light into the dark places, as it were.

A great many seem to regard the securing of the ballot as the supreme attainment and think that with women allowed to vote, everything good will follow as a matter of course. To my mind the ballot is incidental, only a small thing in the work that is before the women of the nation. If politics are not what they should be, if there is graft in places of trust and if there are unjust laws, the men who are responsible are largely what their mothers have made them and their wives usually have finished the job. Perhaps that sounds as if I were claiming for the women a great deal of influence, but trace out a few instances for yourself, without being deceived by appearances, and see if you do not agree with me.

During the controversy between Dr. Cook and Commodore Perry[2] over the discovery of the north pole, the subject was being discussed in a home where I happened to be. It was when Cook was being paid such a high price for his lectures and the mother of two young men present exclaimed, "It makes no difference whether Cook is faking or not! He's getting the money, isn't he, and that's what counts!" She was a woman of whom one expected better things, a refined, educated woman and a devout church member, but her influence on her boys would teach them that money was what counted, regardless of truth or honor.

A young friend with whom I talked the other day said that life was so "much more interesting" to her since she "began to look below the surface of things and see what was beneath." There are deeps beyond deeps in the life of this wonderful world of ours. Let's help the children to see them instead of letting them grow up like the man of whom the poet wrote,

> A primrose by the river's brim
> A yellow primrose was to him and nothing more.

Let's train them, instead, to find "books in the running brooks, sermons in stones and good in everything."

But have you seen any fairies lately, or have you allowed the harsher facts of life to dull your "seeing eye?"

> The sunshine fairies cannot rest
> When evening bells are rung;
> Nor can they sleep in flowers
> When bedtime songs are sung.
>
> They are such busy fairies,
> Their work is never done,
> For all around and round the world
> They travel with the sun.

And while you're soundly sleeping,
They do the best they can
A-painting cherry blossoms
In far away Japan.

The poppy fields of China,
With blossoms bright and gay,
They color on their journey—
And then pass on their way.

And all the happy children,
In islands of the sea,
Know little Ray O'Sunshine,
Who plays with you and me.

When is a Settler an Old Settler?

"Why you are an old settler." said a new comer to us recently. "Yess," [sic] I replied proudly, "we consider ourselves natives," yet when we drove into the Ozarks 20 years ago, with a covered hack and a pony team, we found the "old settler" already here. In conversation with us he made the remark: "My father was an old settler here. He came up from Tennessee before the war."[3] Since then, in working the fields, we have found now and then a stone arrow or spear head made by a settler older still.[4]

When we came to the Ozarks a team of fairly good horses would trade for 40 acres of land. The fences were all rail fences and a great many of the houses were built of logs. The country was a queer mixture of an old and a new country. A great many of the fields had been cropped continually since the war and were so worn out that as one of the neighbors said, "You can't hardly raise an umbrella over it." Aside from these old fields the land was covered with timber and used for range. The "old settlers" told us that the thick growth of timber was comparatively a new thing; that before the country was so thickly settled there were only a few scattering large trees. The fires were allowed to run out and they kept down the young growth of timber. Wild grass grew rankly over all the hills and cattle pastured free.

It has always been a great pleasure to hear tales of earlier days. A neighbor, Mrs. Cleaver, told us stories of her experience in war times and the days, equally as bad which immediately followed. Her husband did not go to the war but one night a band of men came and took him away. She never knew what became of him. Then came hard days for her and her young step-son. They raised a little crop and a hog or two for their living but whenever they had stored a little corn or meat some of the lawless bands of raiders that infested the Ozark hills, would come and take it from them. When the war ended, some of the leaders of these lawless bands continued their depredations,[5] only in a little different fashion. Thru the machinations of one of them, Mrs. Cleaver's step-son was taken from her, by due process of law, and bound out to him until the boy should be of age, to work without wages, of course. When Mrs. Cleaver protested, I suppose in a rather frantic way, she was driven from the court house, with a horse whip, by the sheriff.

Not all the old time stories were so serious. There is the story of the green country boy who never had seen a carpeted floor. A new family moved in from the North somewhere and this boy went to the house one day. As he started to enter the door he saw the carpet on the floor. Standing in the door he swung his long arms and jumped clear across the small room landing on the hearth before the fireplace. Turning to the astonished woman of the house he exclaimed: "Who Mam! I mighty nigh stepped on your kiverled!" Our friend in telling this story always ended with: "I never could make out whether that boy was as big a fool as he pretended to be or not. He made a mighty smart business man when he was older and made the business men of Kansas City and St. Louis hustle to keep up with him," which is a way the hill boys have.

One old lady, who has lived here since the war, says that when she came the "old settlers" told her of the time when a band of Spanish adventurers came up the Mississippi river and wandered thru the Ozarks.[6] Somewhere among the hills they hid their treasure in a cave and it never has been discovered to this day.

But how old must a settler be to be an "old settler" or if you prefer the famous question, "How old is Ann?"

Our Grand Old Men—and Women

EXTRACTS FROM A VISIT WITH MISSOURI'S PIONEER FARM FOLKS
BY JOHN F. CASE

LYDIA KAY: 90 YEARS ON ONE FARM

More than 90 years ago a girl baby came to brighten the farm home of James Howard in Moniteau county, at that time part of Cole county. The little one was named Lydia and she still lives on the same farm. Dense forest surrounded the cabin home and prowling beasts were numerous. Pioneer Howard tilled the soil as best he could and supplied the table with game which could be had in plenty within gunshot from the house. Mr. Howard was a Tennessean but James Kay who married the daughter Lydia, came from Virginia. The young folks built a log house on the Howard farm and lived there until the farm was purchased in later years. To them were born four boys and two girls all of whom were reared to manhood and womanhood. Mrs. Kay's husband died 53 years ago but she kept her brood together, improved the farm and now lives in a modern house, cared for by her youngest son.

"Grandma Kay wasn't lonesome in the old days," says Mrs. Andrew Howard of California, Mo., who sent in the information, "but she gets lonely now. She sits in her rocker and dreams of the past. She has a large comfortable room of her own, and she tells about the early days when her home was a log house with a stick chimney and a fireplace. Families of a dozen children were reared in a 1-room cabin home. Grandma Kay has lived to see the primitive machinery used for planting and harvesting replaced by modern machinery, and the ox team give way first to the steam engine and now to the motor car which daily passes her door. The country was infested with distilleries but today even the saloon has been outlawed. Almost all the timber has disappeared. Her son must secure firewood from neighboring farms. No person in her family has died since

Mr. Kay died 53 years ago. The picture [accompanying the original article] is very good of her altho taken some time ago. She still is hale and hearty and enjoying extra good health."

JOHN R. MAIZE: SPRY AT 94, AND HE CAN BOAST OF 67 YEARS CONTINUOUS RESIDENCE ON HIS HARRISON COUNTY FARM.

"John R. Maize is one of Harrison county's oldest settlers," asserts L.S. Flint of Bethany who sent in the excellent photo showing Grandpa Maize just as he had alighted from his pony after riding 4 miles to the Flint home. "If he lives until August 5 he will be 94 years old. He settled on his farm in 1849, rearing a family of 9 children, all of whom are married and doing well. His memory is excellent and his health is fairly good. Grandma Maize died in 1892 and Grandpa Maize has lived alone on his farm since that time. He has the farm rented." Show me another farmer 94 years old who still manages his farm and his business affairs.

Showing Dad the Way

MANSFIELD HAS A BOYS' GOOD ROAD CLUB THAT WORKS AND PLAYS

Here Laura gives a brief sketch of the topography of the Mansfield region, and explains how a pioneering style of communal activity has given the area an excellent road system.

The science of road making was brought to such perfection in the days of ancient Rome, that some of the old Roman roadways are in existence today. But it remained for the Ozark Mountain town of Mansfield, in the year 1915, to show the world something new in the way of road building.

Mansfield is situated on one of the highest points of the Ozarks, so exactly at the crest of the slopes to the north and south that the rainfall from the eaves, on the north side of the railway station, runs north to the Gasconade river, which drains the northern slopes of the Ozarks, while the rain that falls on the south side of the station roof, finds its way south to Bryant river which is the waterway for the southern slope.

Steep hillsides and swift flowing mountain streams make beautiful scenery but also they make it very hard to keep the roads in fit condition to be traveled and last summer a new element entered into the problem—the urge of competition.

One of the proposed routes, for the state automobile road, runs thru Mansfield and consequently the citizens of the town and surrounding country had quite a severe attack of roadmaking fever.

Other places were affected also and there was a strong, tho friendly rivalry, among the nearby towns and different road districts, as to which should make the best showing in working the roads.

Then the mayor of Mansfield, Dr. F.H. Riley, had an idea. He has an idea every once in a while, but this has proved to be one of the happiest,—"Why not make use of the energy and activity of the boys of the road district, which were going to waste?

"Growing boys must have some excitement. They must have an outlet for their exuberant spirits and some way to work off their superfluous energy. Without proper guidance these things run riot and make trouble for themselves and all concerned. I have it! We will guide this energy and it shall help to turn the wheels of industry even as do the swift streams of the Ozarks, when properly controlled."

Mansfield is a town with only 900 inhabitants but they are very much alive and quite capable of following an idea to see where it will lead, so the "Mansfield Boys Good Road Club" was organized with 50 members and started out to help work the road.

It is astonishing how much work 50 good lively boys can do in a day when their hearts are in it. They raked the loose rocks out of the road; cleaned out ditches and culverts; picked up rocks from adjoining fields to be used on the road; cut brush from the roadway; and thoroly enjoyed it all.

Especially did they enjoy themselves when noontime came, for, with the dinner hour arrived their mothers and their sisters and their aunts, with well filled baskets. And you all know what happens when a small boy meets a picnic.

The boys were not all so small at that—though it made no difference with what happened to the picnic—for the business and professional men of Mansfield, learning what was afoot, had begged to be taken on as associate members of the boys' club. They were present with their picks and shovels and acquired a good appetite for the noontime lunch.

Some of the business men of the town, who were unable to take an active part, opened their purses and contributed to help along the work.

Farmers, who knew of the plans, not to be outdone by the townspeople, came with their teams and gave their own time and strength to the cause.

All worked with great enthusiasm and the spirit of the old time country "workings" and the roads leading into Mansfield presented the appearance of an elongated beehive.

The club spent two days on the road last summer and, besides other work accomplished, the boys themselves picked up and hauled more than 200 loads of rock, which were used in bad places in the road bed and in building a culvert.

The Mansfield Boys Good Roads Club has been a great success, not only in the amount of work accomplished, but because of the example it has set. Which example will be followed, when spring comes, by the organization of several other boys' clubs, for work on the roads of the Ozarks.

As the Mansfield club was the first organized, its members intend to stay in the lead and Dr. Riley and the boys expect to do very much better next summer than they did last. There will be at least one "working" a month, during the summer season, Dr. Riley thinks, and the picnic lunch, at noon, will be a special feature of each occasion.

Being the originator of the plan and one of the three road commissioners for the district, Dr. Riley is in a position to greatly influence the boys of the club and he intends to lead them in beautifying the roads as well as improving their driving condition. He says there is no need for anything to be ugly in order to be useful, and nut and fruit trees, by the roadside, give a pleasant shade on warm days; and make of a road a beautiful driveway. Planting and caring for these trees would be an education in itself for the boys.

Some of the effects of organizing the boys for this work are shown in the increased interest their elders take in the subject of good roads. The Mansfield road district, last fall, voted a bond issue of $20,000 for road work and it is hoped that it will result in putting in good shape the 35 miles of road in the district.

But it is expected that the effects of this work on the boys themselves will be very far reaching. It keeps them occupied during some of their idle time and thus out of mischief: gives them a good, healthy, live interest and makes them feel responsible members of the community.

It teaches them the necessity for good roads; and a proper respect for public property. What boy, after realizing the work it takes to make a good road; and feeling that he owns an interest in it, because of his labors in making it good, but would feel indignant to see the road carelessly or wantonly damaged?

This feeling of a proprietary interest in public property, if wisely handled, will surely extend to other things and help to make these boys, public spirited, intelligent citizens.

Kin-Folks or Relations?

"I do like to have you say kin-folks. It seems to mean so much more than relations or relatives," writes my sister from the North. They do not say kin-folks in the North. It is a Southern expression.

This remark was enough to set me on a train of thought that led me far a-field. Kin-folks! They are such homey-sounding words and strong, too, and sweet. Folks who are akin—why they need not even be relatives or "blood kin!" What a vista that opens up! They are scattered all over the world, these kin-folks of ours and we will find them wherever we go, folks who are akin to us in thought and belief, in aspirations and ideas, tho our relatives may be far away. Not but what those of our own family may be akin to us also, tho sometimes they are not.

Old Mr. Weeks died last winter. His will left the fine farm to his youngest son, subject to providing a home for his mother so long as she lived. A comparatively small sum of money was left each of the seven other children who were scattered in other states. And now a strange thing happened! We always expect to hear of trouble and quarreling among the heirs, over a will and an estate and in this case we were not disappointed. There was trouble, serious trouble and disagreement. The surprising thing was in the form it took. The youngest son flatly refused to abide by his father's will. He would not take the whole farm for himself! "It was not fair to the others!"

His brothers and sisters refused absolutely to take any share of the farm. "It would not be right," they said, when their brother had made the farm what it was by staying at home and working on it, while they had gone away on their own affairs. Lawyers were even called into the case, not to fight for a larger share for their clients, but to persuade the other party to take more of the property than he wished to take. There is nothing new under the sun we are told, but if anything like this ever happened before it has not been my good fortune to hear of it. The members of this family were surely kin-folks as well as relatives.

Two sisters, Mabel and Kate were left orphans when 18 and 20 years old. There was very little for their support, so as they would be obliged to add to their income in some way they went into a little business of ladies' furnishing goods. All the responsibility was left with Mabel altho they were equal partners and she also did most of the work. Kate seemed to have no sense of honor in business nor of the difference between right and wrong in her dealings with her sister. At last Mabel had a nervous breakdown under the strain and the shock of the sudden death of her fiance. While Mabel was thus out of the way, Kate sold the business, married and left town, and when Mabel recovered she found that the business and her sister were gone, that the account at the bank was overdrawn and a note was about due which had been given by the firm and to which her own name had been forged. Because of the confidence which her honor and honesty inspired, Mabel was able to get credit and make a fresh start. She has paid the debts and is becoming prosperous once more.

Were Mabel and Kate Kin-folks? Oh no, merely relatives!

Just a Question of Tact

EVERY PERSON HAS SAID THINGS THEY DIDN'T MEAN

"You have so much tact and can get along with people so well," said a friend of mine once. Then after a thoughtful pause she added, "But I never could see any difference between tact and trickery." Upon my assuring her that there was no difference, she pursued the subject further.

"Now I have no tact whatever, but speak plainly," she said pridefully. "The Scotch people are, I think, the most tactful and the Scotch, you know, are the trickiest nation in the world."

As I am of Scotch descent, I could restrain my merriment no longer and when I recovered enough to say, "You are right, I am Scotch," she smiled ruefully and said, "I told you I had no tact."

Tact does for life what lubricating oil does for machinery. It makes the wheels run smoothly and without it there is a great deal of friction and possibly a breakdown. Many a car on the way of life fails to make the trip as expected for want of lubricant. Tact is a quality that may be acquired. It is only the other way of seeing and presenting a subject. There are always two sides to a thing, you know, and if one side is disagreeable the reverse is quite apt to be very pleasant. The tactful person may see both sides but uses the pleasant one.

"Your teeth are so pretty when you keep them white," said Ida to Stella; which of course was equal to saying that Stella's teeth were ugly when she did not keep them clean, as frequently happened, but Stella left her friend with the feeling that she had been complimented and also with the shamed resolve that she would keep those pretty teeth white.

Tom's shoulders were becoming inclined to droop a little. To be sure he was older than he used to be and sometimes very tired, but the droop was really caused more by carelessness than by anything else. When Jane came home from a visit to a friend whose husband was very round shouldered indeed, she noticed more plainly than usual the beginning of the habit in Tom.

Choosing a moment when he straightened to his full height and squared his shoulders, she said: "Oh Tom! I'm so glad you are tall and straight, not round shouldered like Dick. He is growing worse every day until it is becoming a positive deformity with him." And Tom was glad she had not observed the tendency in his shoulders and thereafter their straightness was noticeable.

Jane might have chosen a moment when Tom's shoulders were drooping and with perfect truthfulness have said: "Tom! You are getting to be round shouldered and ugly like Dick. In a little while you will look like a hunchback."

Tom would have felt hurt and resentful and probably would have retorted, "Well, you're getting older and uglier too," or something like that, and his hurt pride and vanity would have been a hindrance instead of a help to improvement.

The children, of course, get their bad tempers from their fathers, but I think we get our vanity from Adam, for we all have it, men and women alike, and like most things it is good when rightly used.

Tact may be trickery but after all I think I prefer the dictionary definition— "nice discernment." To be tactful one has only to discern or distinguish, or in other words to see nicely and speak and act accordingly.

My sympathy just now, however, is very much with the persons who seem to be unable to say the right thing at the proper time. In spite of oneself there are times when one's mental fingers seem to be all thumbs. At a little gathering, not long ago, I differed with the hostess on a question which arose and disagreed with just a shade more warmth than I intended. I resolved to make it up by being a little extra sweet to her before I left. The refreshments served were so dainty and delicious that I thought I would find some pleasanter way to tell her so. But alas! As it was a very hot day, ice water was served after the little luncheon and I found myself looking sweetly into my hostess's face and heard myself say, "Oh, wasn't that water good." What could one do after that, but murmur the conventional, "Such a pleasant afternoon," at leaving and depart feeling like a little girl who has blundered at her first party.

Our Fair and Other Things

The annual fair at Mansfield was a success in spite the summer's drouth. Farmers surely are the most optimistic people in the world! Altho badly punished, in the conflict with the forces of nature this season, they were by no means defeated, as was proved by the agricultural exhibits and everywhere could be overheard planning for next year's campaign.

Discouraged? Not a bit of it! "It's been a bad season but we'll come out all right," said one man. "The old cows will take us thru." One could understand his confidence after looking at the stock exhibited. Purebred Jerseys, Holsteins and Polled Durhams were there, each so good in its way that one could not be partial to any. In the hog pens were fine Duroc Jerseys and Poland Chinas, one weighing 800 pounds. It looked as tho the day of the "hazel splitter"[7] was past in the Ozarks.

The women as usual did their part toward the fair in a very satisfactory manner in every department. Mrs. C.A. Durnell of Hillside Poultry Farm made a good superintendent of poultry and M.L. Andrews, poultry judge, is conceded to be one of the best in the state. Mr. Andrews is very helpful to anyone interested in poultry. As he examined bird after bird, he displayed their fine points and explained where they failed to come up to standard, to a small interested audience which followed him from coop to coop. Altogether we people of Mansfield feel very proud of our fair.

One amusement feature provided as a free show on the street was, to me, shocking. I knew of course that the thing is often done, but I never have watched while knives were thrown around a human target. The target as usual was a woman and a man threw the knives. Effacing myself behind a convenient corner, which hid the spectacle, I watched the faces of the crowd. They reminded me strongly of the faces of the crowd watching a Mexican bull fight that I saw in a moving picture. There happened to be no bloodshed in the knife throwing but judging by the expression on some of the faces there was a tense expectancy and unconsciously almost a hope that there might be. In the crowd were women and children as well as men and boys, all eager, alert, and watching—for what? A failure of nerve, perhaps, in one of the performers: an instant's dimming of vision or slight miscalculation on the part of the man. There is something thrilling and ennobling in seeing a person brave death in a good cause or for an ideal, but to watch anyone risk being butchered merely to make holiday sport savors too much of other things. We condemn the bull fight and the spectators you know. Is it perhaps a case of the pot calling the kettle black?

It is not alone "one touch of nature" which "makes the whole world kin," but every emotion which writes itself on the human countenance creates a family likeness, with others of its kind, even between people of different races. I saw this plainly when present at a Chinese Salvation Army meeting on a street corner in San Francisco's Chinatown. The crowd was large and all Chinese except myself and escort. Altho Chinese was the only language spoken and I could not understand a word, I could follow the exhorter's meaning and by the expressions on the faces about me could tell the state of mind of his audience. It was one of my many curious experiences in the city and when the leader started singing "Onward Christian Soldiers," in Chinese and the crowd joined in, I felt as tho my ears must be bewitched. It was quite as startling as it was to see the words "Methodist Episcopal Church" over the door of a beautiful building, built in Chinese style, on another street corner in Chinatown. The words seemed no more to belong with the fanciful Chinese architecture than the Chinese words belonged with the good old American hymn tune sung by Oriental folks.

Learning to Work Together

The Bryant Farmers' Club held their first annual auction and stock sale November 2. This plan of an auction sale for a neighborhood is something new, I think, in the work of farmers' clubs. The idea originated in the mind of the president, M.L. Andrews[8] and was eagerly adopted by the club members.

Every member listed what he had for sale and it was surprising how a little from everyone mounted up in the total. There were 40 head of stock listed and a wagon load of household goods.

The day of the auction was pleasant and the old mill yard and the one street of the little town of Bryant were filled with wagons, buggies, horses and motor cars, while a lively crowd of about 400 men, women and children surrounded the auctioneer as he cried the sale, or gathered at the lunch counter for refreshment.

The sale was a success, considering the fact that it was the first of the kind and rather an experiment, it went off very well indeed. The members and officers of the club are learning from experience, however, and already plans are being made to insure that next year's sale shall be more satisfactory still. Some farmers are saying that, if they can list their stock together to sell at auction, there is nothing to hinder their shipping together in carload lots to market. And so the idea of co-operation keeps growing, when once it has taken root.

I know a little band of friends that calls itself a woman's club. The avowed purpose of this club is study, but there is an undercurrent of deeper, truer things than even culture and self improvement. There is no obligation and there are no promises, but in forming the club and in selecting new members, only those are chosen who are kind hearted and dependable as well as the possessors of a certain degree of intelligence and a small amount of that genius which is the capacity for careful work. In short, those who are taken into membership are those who will make good friends and so they are a little band who are each for all and all for each.

If one needs the helping hand of comradeship, not one but all are eager and willing to help, with financial aid if needed, but more often with a good word or a small act of kindness. They are getting so in the habit of speaking good words that I expect to see them all develop into Golden Gossips. Ever hear of golden gossip? I read of it some years ago. A woman who was always talking about her friends and neighbors, made it her business to talk of them in fact, never said anything but good of them. She was a gossip but it was "golden gossip." This woman's club seems to be working in the same way and associations of friendship and mutual helpfulness are being built up which will last for life. It is a beautiful thing and more than ever one is impressed with the idea that it is a pity there are—

> So many gods, so many creeds,
> So many paths that wind and wind
> When just the art of being kind
> Is all the sad world needs.

"Money is the root of all evil" says the proverb, but I think that proverb maker only dug down part way around the plant of evil. If he had really gotten to the root of the matter, I am sure he would have found that root to be selfishness— just selfishness pure and simple. Why all the mad scramble for money? Why are we all "money-mad Americans?" It is just for our selfish gratification with things that money can buy, from world dominion to a stick of striped candy— selfishness, just selfishness.

Not long ago I was visiting in a family where there were several children. The father lost his memorandum book and was inquiring for it. No one had seen it. "I wish," he said, "that you children would find it for me before I come back at noon." There was silence for a minute and then one of the children said: "Why don't you put up a quarter? That'll find it!"

"Well, I will," his father answered and at once the children were all eagerness to search. It seemed to me such a pity to appeal to a selfish interest in the home where there should be loving service, freely given.

In the blacksmith shop, one hot day last summer, the blacksmith was sweating over his hot irons when two idle boys sauntered in and over to the water bucket. It was empty. "Ain't yuh got no water?" asked one of the boys.

"Not if the bucket is empty," answered the blacksmith.

Then the man, for whom the blacksmith was working, spoke up. "Why don't you go get a bucket of water?" he asked.

"I will for a nickel," said the boy.

"Yes, we'll go for a nickel," agreed the other boy.

"Were you going to pay for your drink?" asked the man innocently and the boys looked at him surprised and then slunk away, without filling the bucket. Just an example of selfishness made more contemptible by being so plainly unfair.

Co-operation, helpfulness and fair dealing are so badly needed in the world and if they are not learned as children at home it is difficult for grownups to have a working knowledge of them.

So much depends on starting the children right!

What's in a Word?

A group of friends was gathered around a glowing fire the other evening. The cold outside and the warmth and cheer and soft lights within had opened their hearts and they were talking freely together as good friends should.

"I propose that we eliminate the word can't from our vocabularies for the coming year," said Mrs. Betty. "There ain't no such animile anyhow."

"But sometimes we just c——" began Sister Sue, then stopped abruptly at the sound of an amused chuckle.

"Oh, well—if you feel that way about it!" rejoined Mrs. Betty, "but I still insist that if you see such an animal it is only a creature of the imagination. When I went to school they tried to teach me that it was noble to say, 'I'll try' when confronted with a difficult thing to be done, but it always sounded weak to me. Why! the very expression presupposes failure," she went on with growing earnestness. "Why not say I will and then make good? One can, you know, for if there is not one way to do a thing there are usually two."

"That word 'can't' with its suggestion of failure!" exclaimed George. "Do you know a man came up to me on the street the other day and said, 'You can't lend me a dollar, can you?' He expected to fail in his request—and he most certainly did," he added grimly.

"After all," said brother James slowly, "people do a good deal as they are expected to do, even to saying the things they are expected to say. The power of suggestion is very strong. Did you ever notice how everyone will agree with you about the weather? I have tried it out many a time just for fun. Before the days of motor cars, when we could speak as we passed driving along the road, I have said to the first man I met, 'This is a fine day,' and regardless of what the weather might be, he never would fail to answer, 'Sure, it's a fine day,' or something to that effect and pass on smiling. To the next man I met I would say 'Cold weather we're having,' and his reply would always be, 'Coldest I ever knew at this season,' or 'Mighty cold this morning,' and he would go on his way shivering. No matter if it's raining a man usually will agree with you that it's awfully dry weather, if you suggest it to him right."

"Speaking of friends," said Philip, which no one had been doing tho all could trace the connecting thought, "Speaking of friends,—I heard a man say not long ago that he could count all the friends he had on the fingers of one hand. I wonder"—and his voice trailed off into silence as his thought carried him away. A chorus of protest arose.

"Oh, how awful!" exclaimed Pansy, with the tender eyes. "Anyone has more friends than that. Why, if everybody is sick or in trouble everybody is his friend."

"It all depends on one's definition of friend," said Mrs. Betty in a considering tone. "What do we mean when we say 'friend?' What is the test for a friend?" A silence fell upon the little group around the glowing fire.

"But I want to know," insisted Mrs. Betty. "What is the test for a friend? Just what do you mean Philip, when you say, 'He is my friend?'"

"Well," Philip replied, "when a man is my friend I expect he will stand by me in trouble, that he will do whatever he can to help me if I am needing help and do it at once even at cost of inconvenience to himself."

"Now, Pansy! How do you know your friends?" still insisted Mrs. Betty.

"My friends," said Pansy, with the tender eyes, "will like me anyway, no matter what my faults are. They will let me do as I please and not try to change me but will be my friends whatever I do."

"Next," began Mrs. Betty, but there were exclamations from every side. "No! No! It's your turn now! We want to know what your test of friendship is!"

"Why! I was just asking for information," answered Mrs. Betty with a brilliant smile, the warmth of which included the whole circle. "I wanted to know—

"Tell us! Tell us!" they all insisted.

"Well, then," earnestly, "my friends will stand by me in trouble. They will love me even when I make mistakes and in spite of my faults, but if they see me in danger of taking the wrong course they will warn me. If necessary, they will even tell me of a fault which is perhaps growing on me unaware. One should dare anything for a friend, you know."

"Yes, but to tell friends of a fault is dangerous," said gentle Rosemary. "It is so likely to make them angry."

"To be sure," Mrs. Betty answered. "But if we are a friend we will take it thankfully for the sake of the spirit in which it is given, as we do a Christmas present which otherwise we would not care for."

"Remember well and bear in mind, a constant friend is hard to find, and when you find one good and true, change not the old one for the new," quoted Philip as the group began to break up.

"No, don't change 'em," said George, in the bustle of the putting on of wraps. "Don't change 'em! Just take 'em all in!"

Giving and Taking Advice

I have just learned something new! Isn't it a wonderful thing that we are "never too old to learn" and also sometimes isn't it strange that no matter how many years we have numbered we still learn best from that old, old teacher Experience? For instance, there was the time I read, (not in a farm paper) that the addition of a little vinegar to the lard in which doughnuts were fried would keep them from soaking fat. I was preparing a company dinner not long afterward, and wishing to have my doughnuts especially good, was about to pour the vinegar into the lard when the Man of the Place came into the kitchen. From long association with the cook, he knew that she was doing something different and demanded to know why. When I had explained, he advised me not to try any experiments at that particular time. "Oh, it will be alright," I answered easily, "or it would not have been in that paper." I added the vinegar and learned it was perfectly true that the doughnuts would not soak the grease.

They would hardly soak anything they were so tough.

Experience had taught me one more lesson!

It is so easy to give advice. It is one thing with which the most of us are well supplied and are perfectly willing to part. Sometimes I think we are too quick to do this, too free in handing out unasked an inferior article. There is no way of estimating the mischief done by the well meant but ill-considered advice of friends and acquaintances. Knowing only one side of a question, seeing imperfectly a part of a situation, we say: "Well I wouldn't stand for that a minute," or "You'll be foolish if you do," or "I would" do this or that and go light heartedly on our way never thinking that by a careless word or two we may have altered the whole course of human lives, for some persons will take advice and use it.

There were once two men who had different ways of treating their horses when they went around them in the barn. One always spoke to his horses as he passed so that they might know he was there and not kick. The other never spoke to them. He said it was their business to look before they kicked. This last man often spoke of his way as being much the best. One day he advised the other to change his way of doing because one day he would forget to speak and get kicked. Not long after this actually happened and the man was seriously injured. His wife said to me, "If he had spoken to the horse when he went into the barn as he used to do he would not have been hurt, but lately he has stopped doing that and the horse kicked him before it saw him." I always have thought that the accident happened because of his friend's advice and I have seen so often where what was best for me might not be just the thing for the other fellow that I have decided to keep my advice until asked for and then administer it in small doses.

There are ways of profiting by the experience of others, besides taking advice carelessly given. We might watch, you know, while some one else tried the vinegar on the doughnuts. And that brings me back where I started to tell of the new thing I had learned. It is a great help with the work of sewing to cover the tread of the sewing machine with a piece of soft, thick carpet. The carpet will act as a cushion and one's feet will not become so tired as they otherwise would when using the machine a great deal. There is another advantage in the use of the carpet in cold weather as it is much warmer for the feet to rest on than the cold iron of the machine.

Are You Going Ahead?

"I cannot stand still in my work. If I do not keep studying and going ahead, I slip back," said a friend the other day.

"Well, neither can I in my work," I thought. My mind kept dwelling on the idea. Was there a work that one could learn to do with a certain degree of excellence, and then keep that perfection without a ceaseless effort to advance?

How easy and delightful life might be if we could do this, if when we had attained the position we wished we might rest on our oars and watch the ripples on the stream of life.

Turning my mind resolutely from the picture of what would happen to the person who rested on his oars, expecting to hold his position where the tide was rippling, I began looking around for that place in life where one could stand still, without troubling to advance and without losing what already had been gained.

My friend who plays the piano so beautifully was a fair performer years ago, but has improved greatly as time went by. She spends several hours every day at the instrument practicing. "I have to practice," she says, "or I shall lose my power of execution," and because she does practice to keep what she already has, she goes on improving from day to day and from year to year.

In contrast to this, is the other friend who used to sing so much and who had such a lovely voice. She hardly ever sings now and told me the other day that she thought she was losing her voice. She also said that she was so busy she had no time to practice.

There is also the woman who "completed her education" some years ago. She thought there was no need for further effort along that line and that she had her education for all time, so she settled down to the house work and the poultry. She has read very little of anything that would help her to keep abreast of the times and does not now give the impression of being an educated, cultured person but quite the reverse. No doubt she has forgotten more than I ever knew, but the point is that she has lost it. Refusing to go ahead, she has dropped back.

Even a housekeeper who is a good housekeeper and stays such becomes a better and more capable one from the practice and exercise of her art and profession. If she does not, you may be sure she is slipping back and instead of being proficient will soon be careless, a woman who will say, "I used to be a good housekeeper, but,—"

The same rule applies to character. Our friends and neighbors are either better friends and neighbors today than they were several years ago or they are not so good. We are either broader minded, more tolerant and sympathetic now than we used to be or the reverse is true. The person who is selfish, or mean and miserly—does he not grow more so as the years pass, unless he makes a special effort to go in the other direction?

Our graces are either growing or shrinking. It seems to be a law of nature that everything and every person must move along. There is no standing still. The moment that growth stops, decay sets in.

One of the greatest safeguards against becoming old is to keep growing mentally, you know.

If we do not strive to gain we lose what we already have, for just so surely as "practice makes perfect," the want of practice or the lack of exercise of talents and knowledge makes for the opposite condition.

We must advance or we slip back and few of us are bright enough to turn a slip to good account as did the school boy of long ago. This particular boy was late at school one icy winter morning and the teacher reproved him and asked the reason for his tardiness.

"I started early enough," answered Tom, "but it was so slippery that every time I took one step ahead I slipped back two steps."

There was a hush of astonishment and then the teacher asked, "But if that is true, how did you ever get here?"

"Oh, that's easy," replied Tom. "I was afraid I was going to be late and so I just turned around and came backwards."

Buy Goods Worth the Price

We were speaking of a woman in the community who was ignoring the conventions, thereby bringing joy to the gossips' hearts and a shock to those persons who always think first of what people will say.

"Well of course," said my friend, "it is all perfectly harmless and she has the satisfaction of doing as she pleases, but I'm wondering whether it's worth the price."

There are very few things in this world that we may not have if we are willing to pay their price. You know it has been said that "Every man has his price," which may or may not be true, but without doubt nearly every other thing has its market value and we may make our choice and buy. We must pay, in one way or another, a greater or less amount for everything we have and sometimes we show very poor judgment in our purchases.

Many a woman and girl has paid her good eyesight for a few pieces of hand embroidery or her peace of mind for a new gown, while many a man's good health or good standing in the community, goes to pay for his indulgence in a bad habit.

Is there something in life that you want very much? Then pay the price and take it, but never expect to have a charge account and avoid paying the bills. Life is a good collecter [sic] and sooner or later the account must be paid in full. I know a woman who is paying a debt of this kind on the installment plan. She wanted to be a musician and so she turned her children into the streets and neglected her husband that she might have more time for practice. She already has paid too high a price for her musical education and the worst of it is that she will keep on paying the installments for the rest of her life.

There are persons who act as if the things life has to offer were on sale at an auction and if someone else is likely to secure an article, they will raise their bid without regard to the value of the goods on sale. Indeed the most of us are like people at an auction sale in this respect, that during the excitement and rivalry we buy many things we do not need, nor want, nor know just what to do with, and we pay for them much more than they are worth.

Is it your ambition to outshine your neighbors and friends? Then you are the foolish bidder at the auction sale, raising your bid just because someone else is bidding. I knew a man like this. He owned a motor car of the same size and make as those his friends had but decided he would buy a larger, more powerful, and much more expensive one. His old car was good enough for all his needs, he said, but he was going to have a car that would be "better than the other fellow's." I suppose he figured the cost of the car in dollars and cents, but the real price he paid was his integrity and business honor, and for a bonus, an old and valued friendship. He had very poor judgment as a buyer in my opinion.

Do you desire an education? No matter who pays the money for this, you cannot have it unless you also pay with long hours of study and application.

Do you wish to be popular? Then there is a chance to buy the real lasting thing which means to be well thought of and beloved by people worth while, or the shoddy imitation, a cheap popularity of the "hail fellow well met" sort depending mostly on one's ability to tell a good story and the amount one is able to spend on so called pleasure. As always, the best is the cheapest, for poor goods are dear at any price. The square dealing, the kindness and consideration for others, the helpfulness and love which we must spend if we wish lasting esteem enrich us in the paying besides bringing us what we so much desired. On the other hand, in buying a cheap popularity, people sometimes bankrupt themselves in things, the value of which cannot be estimated. If popular favor must be paid for by the surrender of principles or loss in character, then indeed the price is too high.

Just Neighbors

"Mr. Skelton," the world-class borrower in this article, appears almost identically, but under the name of Ole Larsen, in chapter 1 of *The First Four Years*. There, Laura says that Almanzo was more tolerant than she of Larsen's borrowing, because "one must be neighborly."

There are two vacant places in our neighborhood. Two neighbors have gone ahead on "the great adventure."

We become so accustomed to our neighbors and friends that we take their presence as a matter of course forgetting that the time in which we may enjoy their companionship is limited, and when they are no longer in their places there is always a little shock of surprise mingled with our grief.

When we came to Ozarks more than 20 years ago, Neighbor Deaver was one of the first to welcome us to our new home and now he has moved on ahead to that far country from which no traveler returns. Speaking of Mrs. Case's illness and death, a young woman said, "I could not do much to help them but I did what I could, for Mrs. Case was mighty good to me when I was sick." That tells the story. The neighborhood will miss them both for they were good neighbors. What remains to be said? What greater praise could be given?

I wonder if you all know the story of the man who was moving from one place to another because he had such bad neighbors. Just before making the change, he met a man from the neighborhood to which he was going and told him in detail how mean his old neighbors were, so bad in fact that he would not live among them any longer. Then he asked the other man what the neighbors were like in the place to which he was moving. The other man replied, "You will find just the same kind of neighbors where you are going as those you leave behind you."

It is true that we find ourselves reflected in our friends and neighbors to a surprising extent and if we are in the habit of having bad neighbors we are not likely to find better by changing our location. We might as well make good neighbors in our own neighborhood, beginning, as they tell us charity should, at home. If we make good neighbors of ourselves, we likely shall not need to seek new friends in strange places. This would be a tiresome world if everyone were shaped to a pattern of our own cutting and I think we enjoy our neighbors more if we accept them just as they are.

Sometimes it is rather hard to do, for certainly it takes all kinds of neighbors to make a community. We once had a neighbor who borrowed nearly everything on the place. Mr. Skelton was a good borrower but a very poor hand to return anything. As he lived just across a narrow road from us, it was very convenient—for him. He borrowed the hand tools and the farm machinery, the grindstone and the whetstone and the harness and saddles, also groceries and kitchen tools. One day he came over and borrowed my wash boiler in which to heat water for butchering. In a few minutes he returned and making a separate trip for each article, he borrowed both my dishpans, my two butcher knives, the knife sharpener, a couple of buckets, the boards on which to lay the hog, some matches to light his fire, and as an after thought, while the water was heating he came for some salt. There was a fat hog in our pen and I half expected him to come back once more and borrow the hog, but luckily he had a hog of his own. A few days later when I asked to borrow a paper I was told that they never lent their papers. And yet this family were kind neighbors later when we really needed their help.

The Smiths moved in from another state. Their first caller was informed that they did not want their neighbors "to come about them at all," didn't want to be bothered with them. No one knew the reason but all respected their wishes and left them alone. As he was new to the country, Mr. Smith did not make a success of his farming but he was not bothered with friendly advice.

Chasing Thistledown

*D*id you ever chase thistledown? Oh, of course, when you were a child, but I mean since you have been grown! Some of us should be chasing thistledown a good share of the time.

There is an old story, for the truth of which I cannot vouch, which is so good that I am going to take the risk of telling it and if any of you have heard it before it will do no harm to recall it to your minds. A woman once confessed to the priest that she had been gossiping. To her surprise, the priest instructed her to go gather a ripe head of the thistle and scatter the seed on the wind, then to return to him. This she did wondering why she had been told to do so strange a thing, but her penance was only begun, for when she returned the priest, instead of forgiving her fault, he said: "The thistledown is scattered as were your idle words. My daughter, go and gather up the thistledown!"

It is so easy to be careless, and one is so prone to be thoughtless in talking. I told only half of a story the other day heedlessly overlooking the fact that by telling only a part, I left the listeners with a wrong impression of some very kindly persons. Fortunately I saw in time what I had done and I pounced on that thistledown before the wind caught it or else I should have had a chase.

A newcomer in the neighborhood says, "I do like Mrs. Smith! She seems such a fine woman."

"Well y-e-s," we reply, "I've known her a long time," and we leave the new acquaintance wondering what it is we know against Mrs. Smith. We have said nothing against her but we have "damned with faint praise" and a thistle seed is sown on the wind.

The noun "Gossip" is not of the feminine gender. No absolutely not! A man once complained to me of some things that had been said about his wife. "Damn these gossiping women!" he exclaimed. "They do nothing but talk about their neighbors who are better than they. Mrs. Cook spends all her time running around gossiping when she should be taking care of her children. Poor things, they never have enough to eat, by their looks. Her housework is never done and as for her character everybody knows about——" and he launched into an account of an occurrence which certainly sounded very compromising as he told it. I repeated to myself his first remark with the word men in place of the word "women" just to see how it would sound.

And so we say harmful things carelessly; we say unkind things in a spirit of retaliation or in a measure of self-defense to prove that we are no worse than others and the breeze of idle chatter, from many tongues, picks them up, blows them here and there and scatters them to the four corners of the earth. What a crop of thistles they raise! If we were obliged to go gather up the seed before it had time to grow as the woman in the story was told to do, I am afraid we would be even busier than we are.

The busy hands of farm women are growing browner and browner as the season advances. Two country women were in a gathering of town women the other day and the first one there exclaimed to the other as she came in, "Oh! I'm so glad you came! I was thinking of putting my gloves on to cover up my hands, they're so brown."

"Why I'm proud of the tan on my hands," answered the other, "I've enlisted, you know, and my hands show that I'm doing my part."

There is no time for gloves and primping for the enemy is storming the position. There are hawks over the poultry range and insect pests in the garden while the weeds make raids in the night. It is hand to hand fighting on the farms now and sometimes the enemy gains, but the farmers, both men and women, are people of courage. They planted the crops and cold and frosts made a great deal of replanting necessary. They replanted and the floods came so that much of the planting must be done once more, but there is no thought of anything but keeping up the fight.

Put Yourself in his Place

*O*nce upon a time, a crowd of men were working in the woods where they had to do their own cooking. They took turns at being cook and they made a rule that when any one of them found fault with the food provided, that man must take the cook's place, until he in turn was released from the distasteful job by someone's finding fault with his cooking.

This worked very well, with frequent changes in the occupancy of the cook shanty, until the men had learned better than to criticize the food. No one wanted to take the cook's place so they became very careful about what they said and the poor unfortunate who was cooking for the hungry crew saw no chance of escape. He was careless as to how his work was done but no one found fault; he burned the biscuit, then he made the coffee too weak but still no one objected.

At last he cooked a mess of beans and made them as salt as brine. One of the men at supper that night took a huge mouthful of the beans and as he nearly strangled, he exclaimed, "These beans are sure salty!" Then as the eye of the cook, alight with hope, glanced in his direction, he added, "But my, how good they are!"

It is so much easier to find fault with what others do than to do the right thing one's self. Besides, how much pleasanter to let someone else do it. Of course a mere woman is not expected to understand politics in Missouri, but there is no objection to her understanding human nature and it is certainly amusing to watch the effects of the working of human nature on men's political opinions.

I know of some men who were all for the war during President Wilson's first term. "The United States soldiers ought to go down there and take Mexico! A couple of months would do it! The United States should fight if our shipping is interfered with. It would be easily settled." There was much more to the same effect, but now that the fight is on and there is a chance for them to show what they can do, their fighting spirit seems to have evaporated. It was easy to find fault, but rather than do the work themselves, almost anything is good enough. It is the quiet ones who hoped we might be able to keep out of war who are volunteering.

One after another our young men are enlisting. Eight in a body volunteered a few days ago. The war, the terrible, has been something far off, but now it is coming closer home and soon we shall have a more understanding sympathy with those who have been experiencing its horrors for so long. There is nothing quite like experience to give one understanding and nothing more sure than that if we could be in the other fellow's place for awhile we would be less free with our criticisms.

In the days of long ago when armored knights went journeying on prancing steeds, two knights, coming from opposite directions, saw between them a shield standing upright on the ground. As the story goes, these fighting men disagreed about the color of the shield and each was so positive, the one that it was black, and the other that it was white, that from disputing about it they came to blows and charged each other right valiantly. The fury with which they rode their steeds carried each one past the shield to where the other had stood before, and as they turned to face each other again, each saw the side of the shield which the other had first seen and the man who had said the shield was white found the side he was now looking at to be black, while the one who had declared the shield was black found himself facing the white side, so each got the other's point of view and felt very foolish that they had fought over so simple a thing. It makes a difference when you're in the other fellow's place.

Let Us be Just

The story told here is retold in chapter 10 of *Little House in the Big Woods,* where the characters are Laura and her golden-haired sister, Mary.

Two little girls had disagreed, as was to be expected because they were so temperamentally different. They wanted to play in different ways and as they had to play together all operations were stopped while they argued the question. The elder of the two had a sharp tongue and great facility in using it. The other was slow to speak but quick to act and they both did their best according to their abilities.

Said the first little girl: "You've got a snub nose and your hair is just a common brown color. I heard Aunt Lottie say so! Ah! Don't you wish your hair was a be-a-utiful golden like mine and your nose a fine shape? Cousin Louisa said that about me, I heard her!"

The second little girl could not deny these things. Her dark skin, brown hair and snub nose as compared with her sister's lighter coloring and regular features, were a tragedy in her own little life. She could think of nothing cutting to reply for she was not given to seeing unkind things nor was her tongue nimble enough to say them, so she stood digging her bare toes into the ground, hurt, helpless and tongue-tied.

The first little girl, seeing the effect of her words, talked on. "Besides you're two years younger than I am and I know more than you so you have to mind me and do as I say!"

This was too much! Sister was prettier, no answer could be made to that. She was older, it could not be denied, but that gave her no right to command. At last here was her chance to act!

"And you have to mind me," repeated the first little girl. "I will not!" said the second little girl and then, to show her utter contempt for such authority, this little brown girl slapped her elder, golden-haired sister.

I hate to write the end of the story. No, not the end! No story is ever ended! It goes on and on and the effects of this one followed this little girl all her life, showing in her hatred of injustice. I should say that I dislike to tell what came next, for the golden-haired sister ran crying and told what had happened, except her own part in the quarrel, and the little brown girl was severely punished. To be plain she was soundly spanked and set in a corner. She did not cry but sat glowering at the parent who punished her and thinking in her rebellious little mind that when she was large enough she would return the spanking with interest.

It was not the pain of the punishment that hurt so much as the sense of injustice, the knowledge that she had not been treated fairly by one from whom she had the right to expect fair treatment, and that there had been a failure to understand where she had thought a mistake impossible. She had been beaten and bruised by her sister's unkind words and had been unable to reply. She had defended herself in the only way possible for her and felt that she had a perfect right to do so, or if not, then both should have been punished.

Children have a fine sense of justice that sometimes is far truer than that of older persons, and in almost every case, if appealed to, will prove the best help in governing them. When children are ruled thru their sense of justice there are no angry thoughts left to rankle in their minds. Then a punishment is not an injury inflicted on them by someone who is larger and stronger but the inevitable consequence of their own acts and a child's mind will understand this much sooner than one would think. What a help all their lives, in self control and self government this kind of a training would be!

We are prone to put so much emphasis on the desirability of mercy that we overlook the beauties of the principle of justice. The quality of mercy is a gracious, beautiful thing, but with more justice in the world there would be less need for mercy and exact justice is most merciful in the end. The difficulty is that we are so likely to make mistakes we cannot trust our judgment and so must be merciful to offset our own shortcomings, but I feel sure when we are able to comprehend the workings of the principle of justice, we shall find that, instead of being opposed to each other, infallible justice and mercy are one and the same thing.

If We Only Understood

Mrs. Brown was queer. The neighbors all thought so and, what was worse, they all said so.

Mrs. Fuller happened in several times, quite early in the morning and, altho the work was not done up, Mrs. Brown was sitting leisurely in her room or else she would be writing at her desk. Then Mrs. Powers went thru the house one afternoon and the dishes were stacked back unwashed, the beds still airing, and everything "at sixes and sevens," except the room where Mrs. Brown seemed to be idling away her time. Mrs. Powers said Mrs. Brown was "just plain lazy" and she didn't care who heard her say it.

Ida Brown added interesting information when she told her schoolmates, after school, that she must hurry home and do up the work. It was a shame the neighbors said, that Mrs. Brown should idle away her time all day and leave the work for Ida to do after school.

It was learned later that Mrs. Brown had been writing for the papers to earn money to buy Ida's new winter outfit. Ida had been glad to help by doing the work after school so that her mother might have the day for study and writing, but they had not thought it necessary to explain to the neighbors.

I read a little verse a few years ago entitled, "If We Only Understood," and the refrain was:

> "We would love each other better,
> If we only understood."

I have forgotten the author and lost the verse, but the refrain has remained in my memory and comes to my mind every now and then when I hear unkind remarks made about people.

The things that people do would look so differently to us if we only understood the reasons for their actions, nor would we blame them so much for their faults if we knew all the circumstances of their lives. Even their sins might not look so hideous if we could feel what pressure and perhaps suffering had caused them. The safest course is to be as understanding as possible and where our understanding fails call charity to its aid. Learn to distinguish between persons and the things they do, and while we may not always approve of their actions, have a sympathy and feeling of kindness for the persons themselves.

It may even be that what we consider faults and weaknesses in others are only prejudices on our own part. Some of us would like to see everybody fitted to our own pattern and what a tiresome world this would be if that were done. We should be willing to allow others the freedom we demand for ourselves. Everyone has the right to self expression.

If we keep this genial attitude toward the world and the people in it, we will keep our own minds and feelings healthy and clean. Even the vigilance necessary to guard our thoughts this way will bring us rewards in better disciplined minds and happier dispositions.

Keep Journeying On

"Youth longs and manhood strives, but age remembers,
Sits by the raked-up ashes of the past
And spreads its thin hands above the glowing embers
That warm its shivering life blood till the last."

Those lines troubled me a great deal when I first read them. I was very young then and I thought that everything I read in print was the truth. I didn't like it a little bit that the chief end of my life and the sole amusement of my old age should be remembering. Already there were some things in my memory that were not particularly pleasant to think about. I have since learned that few persons have such happy and successful lives that they would wish to spend years in just remembering.

One thing is certain, this melancholy old age will not come upon those who refuse to spend their time indulging in such dreams of the past. Men and women may keep their life blood warm by healthy exercise as long as they keep journeying on instead of sitting by the way trying to keep themselves warm over the ashes of remembrance.

Neither is it a good plan for people to keep telling themselves they are growing old. There is such a thing as a law of mental suggestion that makes the continual affirmation of a thing work toward its becoming an accomplished fact. Why keep suggesting old age until we take on its characteristics as a matter of course? There are things much more interesting to do than keeping tally of the years and watching for infirmities.

I know a woman who when she saw her first gray hair began to bewail the fact that she was growing old and to change her ways to suit her ideas of old age. She couldn't "wear bright colors any more" she was "too old." She must be more quiet now, "it was not becoming in an old person to be so merry." She had not "been feeling well lately" but she supposed she was "as well as could be expected of a person growing old," and so on and on. I never lost the feeling that the years were passing swiftly and that old age was lying in wait for the youngest of us, when in her company.

Of course, no one can really welcome the first gray hair or look upon the first wrinkles as beautiful, but even those things need not affect our happiness. There is no reason why we should not be merry as we grow older. If we learn to look on the bright side while we are young, those little wrinkles at the corners of the eyes will be "laughing wrinkles" instead of "crows feet."

There is nothing in the passing of the years by itself, to cause one to become melancholy. If they have been good years, then the more of them the better. If they have been bad years, be glad they are passed and expect the coming ones to be more to your liking.

Old age is not counted by years anyway. No one thinks of President Wilson as an old man. He is far too busy a person to be thought old, tho some men of his years consider their life work done. Then there is the white-haired "Grandmother of the Revolution" in Russia still in the forefront of events in that country, helping to hold steady a semblance of government and a force to be considered in spite of, or perhaps because of, the many years she has lived. These two are finding plenty to do to keep warmth in their hearts and need no memories for that purpose.

Perhaps after all the poet whose verse I have quoted meant it as a warning that if we did not wish to come to that unlovely old age we must keep on striving for ourselves and for others. There was no age limit set by that other great poet when he wrote,

> "Build thee more stately mansions, oh, my soul
> As the swift seasons roll!"

It is certainly a pleasanter, more worthwhile occupation to keep on building than to be raking up the ashes of dead fires.

What Would You Do?

What would you do if you had a million dollars?

I asked the question once of a young man of my acquaintance. He was the only son of rich parents and been reared like the lilies of the field to "toil not." Then suddenly his father decided that he must learn to work. Working for a salary was supposed to teach him the value of money and learning the business would teach him how to care for his father's property when he should inherit it. But he did not take kindly to the lessons. He had been a butterfly so long he could not settle down to being a busy bee. Office hours came too early in the morning, and why should he keep office hours, anyway, when the fishing and hunting were good?

"Bert," I said to him one day, "what would you do if you had a million dollars?"

Bert looked at me gravely a moment and then, with a twinkle in his eye, said earnestly: "If I had a million dollars I would buy a bulldog, a big brindle one. I would keep him under my office desk and if any one came in and said 'business' to me I would say 'Take him Tige'."

I read in a California paper last week of an altogether different type of man who had arrived at somewhat the same conclusion as Bert, but by exactly the opposite route. This man was an old desert prospector, "desert rat" as they are called in the West, who had spent years hunting for gold in the desert. He came out to the nearest town with his burro and packs after supplies and found that he was heir to a fortune and that there had been quite a search thru the country to find him. He did not want the money and at first refused to take it. But it was his and he must make some disposition of it, so he insisted that a trustee be appointed to take care of it for him.

The old "desert rat," with all his worldly possessions in a pack on the back of a burro, and Bert who had grown to manhood with no wish unsatisfied, that money could gratify, had both come to the same decision—the burden of riches was more than they would bear.

The real character of men and women comes to the surface under stress and sudden riches is as strong a test as any.

Just now there is a chance of fortune coming to unexpected places in the Ozark hills thru the boom in mining operations. Several farm women were talking over the prospects.

"What will you do when they strike it rich on your place?" some one asked.

"Oh! I'll get some new spring clothes and some more Holsteins," answered Mrs. Slade.

"Clothes, of course, but who would stop there?" exclaimed Mrs. Rice. "I shall buy motor cars and diamonds."

"I'll sell out the place and leave these hills," said Mrs. Wade. "How about you, Mrs. Woods?"

"I wouldn't go away," said Mrs. Woods slowly. "I should just like to help and I can help better where I am accustomed to people and things."

Her serious face lighted and her eyes shone as she continued.

"I do so desire to help a little and there is so much one could do with a little money, not just ordinary charity, there are so many persons looking after that, but some playthings for children here and there who do not have any; the pleasures of paying a mortgage now and then, for some hard-working family who could not pay it themselves; just helping those who need it before they become discouraged. It would be so much better than taking care of them after they have given up trying to help themselves. I'm going to do some of these things if they find ore on our place."

And so they showed their different characters and dispositions and the objects of their lives—business and show and snobbishness and love for others with a sincere desire to share good fortune with those less fortunate.

What would you do if you should suddenly become rich? Think out the answer and then look at yourself impartially by the light that answer will throw upon you! It is surprising what an opinion one sometimes forms of one's self by mentally standing off and looking on as at a stranger.

Do the Right Thing Always

"It is always best to treat people right," remarked my lawyer friend.

"Yes, I suppose so, in the end," I replied inanely.

"Oh of course!" he returned, "but that was not what I meant. It pays every time to do the right thing! It pays now and in dollars and cents."

"For instance?" I asked

"Well for the latest instance: a man came to me the other day to bring suit against a neighbor. He had good grounds for damages and could win the suit, but it would cost him more than he could recover. It would make his neighbor expense and increase the bad feeling between them. I needed that attorney's fee, but it would not have been doing the right thing to encourage him to bring suit, so I advised him to settle out of court. He insisted but I refused to take the case. He hired another lawyer, won his case and paid the difference between the damages he recovered and his expenses.

"A client came to me a short time afterward with a suit worth-while and a good retainer's fee, which I could take without robbing him. He was sent to me by the man whose case I had refused to take and because of that very refusal."

Is it possible that "honesty is the best policy" after all, actually and literally? I would take the advice of my lawyer friend on any other business and I have his word on it that it pays to do the right thing here and now.

To do the right thing is simply to be honest, for being honest is more than refraining from short-changing a customer or robbing a neighbor's hen roost. To be sure those items are included, but there is more to honesty than that. There is such a thing as being dishonest when no question of financial gain or loss is involved. When one person robs another of his good name, he is dishonest. When by an unnecessary, unkind act or cross word, one causes another to lose a day or an hour of happiness, is that one not a thief? Many a person robs another of the joy of life while taking pride in his own integrity.

We steal from today to give to tomorrow; we "rob Peter to pay Paul." We are not honest even with ourselves; we rob ourselves of health; we cheat ourselves with sophistries; we even "put an enemy in our mouths to steal away our brains."

If there were a cry of "stop thief!" we would all stand still. Yet nevertheless, in spite of our carelessness, we all know deep in our hearts that it pays to do the right thing, tho it is easy to deceive ourselves for a time. If we do the wrong thing, we are quite likely never to know what we have lost by it. If the lawyer had taken the first case, he might have thought he had gained by so doing, for he never would have known of the larger fee which came to him by taking the other course.

Overcoming Our Difficulties

"A difficulty raiseth the spirit of a great man. He hath a mind to wrestle with it and give it a fall. A man's mind must be very low if the difficulty doth not make part of his pleasure." By the test of these words of Lord Halifax, there are a number of great persons in the world today.

After all, what is a difficulty but a direct challenge? "Here I am in your way," it says, "you cannot get around me nor overcome me! I have blocked your path!" Anyone of spirit will accept the challenge and find some way to get around or over, or thru that obstacle. Yes! And find pleasure in the difficulty for the sheer joy of surmounting it as well as because there has been an opportunity once more to prove one's strength and cunning and by the very use of these qualities cause an increase in them.

The overcoming of one difficulty makes easier the conquering of the next until finally we are almost invincible. Success actually becomes a habit thru the determined overcoming of obstacles as we meet them one by one.

If we are not being successful, if we are more or less on the road toward failure, a change in our fortunes can be brought about by making a start, however small, in the right direction and then following it up. We can form the habit of success by beginning with some project and putting it thru to a successful conclusion however long and hard we must fight to do so; by "wrestling with" one difficulty and "giving it a fall." The next time will be easier.

For some reason, of course according to some universal law, we gather momentum as we proceed in whatever way we go, and just as by overcoming a small difficulty we are more able to conquer the next, tho greater, so if we allow ourselves to fail it is easier to fail the next time and failure becomes a habit until we are unable to look a difficulty fairly in the face, but turn and run from it.

There is no elation equal to the rise of the spirit to meet and overcome a difficulty, not with a foolish over-confidence but keeping things in their proper relations by praying, now and then, the prayer of a good fighter whom I used to know. "Lord make me sufficient to mine own occasion."

Swearing is a Foolish Habit

Laura and her sisters weren't exposed to bad language when they were young. In chapter 6 of *Little House on the Prairie,* "Moving In," Pa comes close to using a mild expletive while he's struggling to cover the cabin roof with canvas in a high wind— but Ma sees what's coming, cautions him, and he catches himself in time. In this article Laura deplores bad language in general, especially among the young, and takes the greatest exception` to blasphemy. She and Almanzo were both regular churchgoers. In De Smet they attended the Congregationalist church, and in Mansfield, Laura, Almanzo and Rose used to go to the Methodist church every Sunday. Laura was also a member of The Eastern Star, a charitable organization, and Almanzo belonged to Mansfield's Masonic Lodge.

I heard a boy swear the other day, and it gave me a distinctly different kind of shock than usual. I had just been reading an article in which our soldiers were called crusaders who were offering themselves, in their youth, as a sacrifice in order that right might prevail against wrong and that those ideals, which are in effect the teachings of Christ, shall be accepted as the law of nations.

When I heard the boy use the name of Christ in an oath, I felt that he had belittled the mighty effort we are making and that he had put an affront upon our brave soldiers by using lightly the name of the great Leader who first taught the principles for which they are dying. The boy had not thought of it in this way at all. He imagined that he was being very bold and witty, quite a grown man in fact.

I wonder how things came to be so reversed, from the right order, that it should be thought daring and smart to swear, instead of being regarded as utterly foolish and a sign of weakness, betraying a lack of self-control. If people could only realize how ridiculous they appear when they call down the wrath of the Creator and Ruler of the Universe just because they have jammed their thumbs, I feel sure they would never be guilty of swearing again. It is so out of proportion, something as foolish and wasteful as it would be to use the long range gun which bombarded Paris, to shoot a fly. If we call upon the Mightiest for trivial things, upon whom or what shall we call in the great moments of life?

There are some things in the world which should be damned to the nethermost regions, but surely it is not some frightened animal whom our own lack of self-control has made rebellious, or an inanimate object that our own carelessness has caused to smite us. Language loses its value when it is so misapplied and in moments of real and great stress or danger we have nothing left to say.

It is almost hopeless to try to reform older persons who have the habit of swearing fastened upon them. Like any other habit, it is difficult to break and it is useless to explain to them that it is a waste of force and nervous energy, but I think we should show the children the absurdity of wasting the big shells of language on small insignificant objects. Perhaps a little ridicule might prick that bubble of conceit and the boy with his mouth full of his first oaths might not feel himself such a dashing, daredevil of a fellow if he feared that he had made himself ridiculous.

When Proverbs Get Together

It had been a busy day and I was very tired, when just as I was dropping off to sleep I remembered that bit of mending I should have done for the man of the place. Then I must have dreamed, for in my fancy, I saw that rent in the garment enlarge and stretch into startlingly large proportions.

At the same time a familiar voice sounded in my ear, "A stitch in time saves nine," it said.

I felt very discouraged indeed at the size of the task before me and very much annoyed that my neglect should have caused it to increase to nine times its original size, when on the other side of me a cheerful voice insinuated, "It is never too late to mend."

Ah! There was that dear old friend of my grandmother who used to encourage her to work until all hours of the night to keep the family clothes in order. I felt impelled to begin at once to mend that lengthened rent, but paused as a voice came to me from a dark corner saying, "A chain is no stronger than its weakest link."

"Shall a man put new wine into old bottles," chimed in another. Of course not, I thought, then why put new cloth——.

But now the voices seemed to come from all about me. They appeared to be disputing and quarreling, or at least disagreeing among themselves.

"Oh what a tangled web we weave when first we practice to deceive," said a smug, oily voice.

"But practice makes perfect," piped a younger voice, sweetly tho with an impudent expression.

"And if at first you don't succeed, try, try again," chirped a small voice with a snicker and it seemed to me that the room was filled with soft laughter.

Evidently thinking that something should be done to put the younger folks in their place, a proverb with a very stern voice spoke from a far corner. "Children should be seen and not heard," he said and a demure little voice at once answered, "Out of the mouth of babes cometh wisdom."

This was really growing interesting. I had not realized that there were so many wise proverbs and that they might fall out among themselves.

Now a couple of voices made themselves heard, evidently continuing a discussion.

"A rolling stone gathers no moss," said a rather disagreeable voice and I caught a shadowy glimpse of a hoary old proverb with a long, gray beard.

"But a setting hen never grows fat," retorted his companion in a sprightly tone.

"An honest man is the most noble work of God," came a high, nasal voice with a self righteous undertone.

"Ah, yes! Honesty is the best policy, you know," came the answer in a brisk business-like tone, just a little cutting.

"A fool and his money are soon parted," said a thin, tight-lipped voice with a puckering quality, I felt sure would draw the purse strings tight.

"Oh, well, money is the root of all evil, why not be rid of it?" answered a jolly, rollicking voice with a hint of laughter in it.

But now there seemed to be danger of a really violent altercation for I heard the words "sowing wild oats," spoken in a cold, sneering tone, while an angry voice retorted hotly, "There is no fool like an old fool," and an admonitory voice added, "It is never too late to mend." Ah! Grandmother's old friend with a different meaning in the words.

Then at my very elbow spoken for my benefit alone, I heard again the words, "It is never too late to mend." Again I had a glimpse of that neglected garment with the rent in it grown to unbelievable size. Must I? At this time of night! But a soft voice whispered in my ear, "Sufficient unto the day is the evil thereof," and with a smile at my grandmother's friend, I drifted into dreamless sleep.

Your Code of Honor

What is you personal code of honor? Just what do you consider dishonorable or disgraceful in personal conduct? It seems to me that we had all grown rather careless in holding ourselves to any code of honor and just a little ashamed of admitting that we had such a standard. At best our rules of life were becoming a little flexible and we had rather a contemptuous memory of the knights of King Arthur's round table who fought so often for their honor and still at times forgot it so completely, while we pitied the Pilgrim Fathers for their stern inflexibility in what they considered the right way of life.

Just now, while such mighty forces of right and wrong are contending in the world, we are overhauling our mental processes a little and finding out some curious things about ourselves. We can all think of examples of different ideas of what is dishonorable. There are the persons who strictly fulfil their given word. To them it would be a disgrace not to do as they agree, not to keep a promise, while others give a promise easily and break their word with even greater ease.

Some persons have a high regard for truth and would feel themselves disgraced if they told a lie, while others prefer a lie even tho the truth were easier.

There are persons who have no scruples to prevent them from eaves-dropping, reading letters not intended for them, or any manner of prying into other persons' private affairs, and to others the doing of such things is in a manner horrifying.

There are scandal-mongers who are so eager to find and scatter to the four winds a bit of unsavory gossip that they are actually guilty in their own souls of the slips in virtue that they imagine in others, and contrasting with these are people so pureminded that they would think themselves disgraced if they entertained in their thoughts such idle gossip.

I know a woman whose standard of honor demands only, "the greatest good to the greatest number, including myself." The difficulty with this is that a finite mind can scarcely know what is good for other persons or even one's self.

Another woman's code of honor is to be fair, to always give the "square deal" to the other person and this is very difficult to do because the judgment is so likely to be partial.

There is a peculiar thing about the people who hold all these differing ideas of what they will allow themselves to do. We seldom wish to live up to the high standard to which we hold the other fellow. The person who will not keep his word becomes very angry if a promise to him is broken. Those who have no regard for truth, in what they say, expect that others will be truthful when talking to them. People who pry into affairs which are none of their business consider the same actions disgraceful in others and gossips think that they should be exempt from the treatment they give to other people. I never knew it to fail and it is very amusing at times to listen to the condemnation of others' actions by one who is even more guilty of the same thing.

It does one good to adhere strictly to a rule of conduct, if that rule is what it should be. Just the exercise of the will in refusing to follow the desires, which do not conform to the standard set, is strengthening to the character, while the determination to do the thing demanded by that standard and the doing of it however difficult, is an exercise for the strengthening of the will power which is far better than anything recommended for that purpose by books.

If you doubt that it pays in cash and other material advantages to have a high code of honor and live up to it, just notice the present plight of the German government. At the beginning of the war they threw away their honor, broke their pledged word and proclaimed to the world that their written agreements were mere scraps of paper. Now when they ask for a conference to discuss a "peace by agreement," the allies reply, in effect, "but an agreement with you would in no sense be binding upon you. We cannot trust again to your word of honor since your signed pledge is a mere 'scrap of paper' and your verbal promises even less."

It is plain, then, that nations are judged by their standards of honor and treated accordingly and it is the same with individuals. We judge them by their code of honor and the way they live up to it. It is impossible to hold two standards, one for ourselves and a different one for others, for what is dishonorable in them would be the same for us and that seems in the end to be the only sure test, embracing and covering all the rest, the highest code of honor yet voiced— "Whatsoever ye would that men should do to you, do ye even so to them!"

Early Training Counts Most

"Don't open that door again, Tom! It lets in too much cold," said Tom's mother, with what I thought was an unnecessarily sharp note in her voice.

It was the first chilly day of early autumn and there was no fire in the house except in the kitchen stove. As I was making an afternoon visit we of course sat in the front room—and shivered. In a moment the outside door opened again and Tom and a gust of raw wind entered together.

"I told you not to open that door! If you do it again I'll spank you good!" said Tom's mother and Tom immediately turned around, opened the door and went out.

We talked on busily for another moment when, feeling more chilly than usual, looked around and saw Tom standing in the open door, swinging it to and fro.

"Tom!" exclaimed his mother, "I told you not to open that door! Come here to me!" As the door swung shut, Tom turned and faced his mother, took a few steps toward her, raised himself on his tiptoes, with his hands behind him and— turned around, opened the door and walked out.

His mother screamed after him, "Tom! If you open that door again, I'll skin you alive!"

"You know you wouldn't do that and Tom knows it too," I said. "Oh, of course," she replied, "but I have to tell him something." I know. Tom's mother is trying to teach her boy to be truthful, but a few days ago he got into mischief and when asked who had done the damage he replied, "Sister did it."

Tom was punished for telling a lie but I imagine it would be rather difficult to explain to him why it was all right to tell a falsehood about what would happen and all wrong to tell one about what had happened; why he should be punished and his mother not.

While I was busy with my work the other morning, a great commotion arose in the dooryard. There was shouting, the dog was barking furiously and there was the noise of running and trampling. I hurried to the door and found several boys in the yard darting here and there, shouting to each other, "Catch it! There is goes!"

As I opened the door a couple of boys put their feet into the meshes of the woven wire fence and climbed over it as tho it had been a stairs, altho the gate was only a few steps from them. Evidently that was the way they had entered the dooryard.

"Boys what are you doing?" I asked. "Oh! Just chasing butterflies," answered one, while another added as tho that excused everything, "Our teacher is just down there," indicating a place well within the fenced field.

When we had taken stock of the damage done by the butterfly chasers we found that the barbed wire fence had been broken down where they had entered the fields and the woven wire fence was badly stretched and sagged. Wire fencing is high these days and help impossible to get so that such raids are particularly annoying just now tho they are not, by any means, anything new.

We are engaged just now in a mighty struggle to teach a certain part of the people of the world a respect for truth and for the rights and property of other people. Are we failing to teach these things at home as we should?

We are told that the reason for the warped national conscience of the German nation is, that the people have been trained from infancy for the things which they have been doing in this war, taught in such a manner that they could be brought to do the awful things which they have done. The results show with startling vividness the effects of childhood impressions and the training of youth.

If in one generation a gentle kind-hearted people can be changed into fiends by a system of teaching, what might be accomplished if children were as carefully trained in the opposite direction. Truly, "As the twig is bent, the tree inclines."

Opportunity

"Grasp opportunity by the forelock, for it is bald behind," says the old proverb. In other words, we must be ready to meet and take advantage of opportunities as they come, or we will lose the chance. We cannot have any hold on them once they have passed by. Nor is time and endeavor spent in preparing ourselves ever wasted, for if we are ready, opportunity is sure to come.

President Wilson is one of the finest examples of a man who was prepared for the opportunity that came to him. In studying his life one comes to feel that he must have decided, while yet a boy, to become President and carefully prepared himself for it, so exactly did his life, up to the time, fit him for the position.

Virtually all his life Wilson was a student of government. He was nearly 30 when his academic training was ended, then a two years' study of law added a practicable equipment. But all these years of hard study were only a beginning for the still more arduous study he did in preparation for the lectures he gave and the magazine articles and books he wrote, mostly on subjects relating to history and legislation.

Before there was any idea of making him President, before he could have seen any likelihood of such a thing, he knew congress and congressional procedure thoroly, far better than did many experienced congressmen.

Wilson's experience as president of Princeton university gave him a training in the handling of men and also in fighting for democratic institutions and so in this great crisis of American history, the opportunity found the man prepared, trained and waiting to take his high place in the world, a position where he is called upon to put to use all the knowledge and skill he acquired in all those long years of study and training.

There are other great persons of whom the same is true. In fact no one can become great who is not ready to take the opportunity when it comes, nor indeed succeed in smaller matters and whatever we prepare ourselves to do or become, the opportunity will come to us to do or become that thing.

Even tho we never become one of the great persons of the world, the chance is sure to come to us to use whatever knowledge we acquire

I knew a woman who denied herself other things in order that she might pay for French lessons. There seemed no chance that it would ever be an advantage to her except as a means of culture, but she now has a good position at a large salary which she would have been unable to fill but for her knowledge of French.

There is unfortunately a reverse side to this picture I have drawn of efforts crowned by success—just as achievements are made possible by a careful preparation, a lack of effort to reach forward and beyond our present position works inversely, and again examples are too numerous to mention.

A hired man on a farm who always needs a boss; who is unable mentally and by disposition to work unless his employer is present and leading; who never fits himself, by being responsible and trustworthy, for the responsibility of owning and running his own farm, will always be a hired man either on a farm or elsewhere.

The tenant farmer who is not preparing himself for being an owner by putting himself mentally in an owners place, getting his point of view and realizing his difficulties, is the tenant farmer who is always having trouble with his landlord and almost never comes to own his own farm. Realizing the difficulties and solving the problems of the next step up seem to lead inevitably to taking that step.

If we do a little less than is required by the position we now fill, whether in our own business or working for someone else; if we do not learn something of the work of the person higher up we are never ready to advance and then we say, "I had a good chance if only I had known how, and so forth."

If we spend on our living every cent of our present income, we are not ready to take that opportunity which requires a little capital and then we say, "that was a good chance if I could only have raised the money."

There is also a touch of humor to be found in the fact that what we prepare for comes to us, altho it is rather pitiful. Humor and pathos are very close "kin."

When the influenza came to our town, Mrs. C. called a friend and tried to engage her to come and nurse her thru the illness.

"Have you the influenza?" asked the friend.

"Oh no!" replied Mrs. C. "None of us has it yet, but I'm all ready for it. I have my bed all clean and ready to crawl into as soon as I feel ill. Everything is ready but a nurse and I want you to come and take care of me."

In a very few days Mrs. C. was in bed with an attack of influenza. She had prepared for the visit and she could say with the psalmist, "The thing I feared has come upon me."

The American Spirit

"The food administration now becomes a great machine of mercy destined to carry the American spirit into the homes and hearts of a great host of bewildered, confused human beings, hungry, discouraged, saddened, submerged by the wreckage resulting from the war. They have gone thru fire for us. The least we can do is to help them to their feet, to see that they are fed and clothed. Don't let your community backslide! Play the game thru! America hates a quitter."

These ringing words were spoken by Dr. Ray Lyman Wilbur, president of Stanford University.

As a nation we have made a great reputation. It now remains to live up to it. Just what is this American spirit that our overseas force of fighters and helpers have carried into Europe? It is a spirit of helpfulness and courage, of sympathy and sacrifice, of energy and of fair play.

We have sent our fighting men to the aid of the wronged and helpless and food and clothing to the starving and destitute. Never before in history have the people of a whole nation denied themselves food that they might feed the hungry of other nations.

I am sure that a great many people felt a sort of flatness and staleness in life when the war ended. Altho they were glad and deeply thankful, there was an unpleasantness in going back to ordinary things, a letting down from the heights to which they had attained, a silence in place of the bugle call to duty, to which their spirits had become attuned.

But there is a chance to exercise still further those qualities which, in spite of all the horrors, have made the war a glorious thing by showing how the good still rises triumphant over the bad in the heart of humanity.

The appeal of Dr. Wilbur comes most appropriately at this time for the American spirit as it has been displayed is really the spirit of Christmas or in other words the spirit of Christianity, a practicable example of loving and serving and giving.

It is a wonderful thing for us to have accepted as our own such national ideals, but we cannot hold them as a nation unless we accept them for our own as individuals. So the responsibility rests upon each of us to keep our country true to the course it has taken and up to the high standard it has reached.

Notes for "The Ways of the World"

1. This spelling seems to reflect the *Ruralist's* (or Laura's) belated falling into line with Theodore Roosevelt's 1906 Executive Order directing the Government Printing Office to follow Simplified Spelling guidelines affecting some 300 words, including "thru." In this Roosevelt was following a proposal outlined in Noah Webster's 1783 American Spelling and Grammar.

2. Here Laura's pen slips. She refers not to Commodore Matthew Calbraith Perry (1794–1858), who opened Japan to American trade in 1854, but to Admiral Robert Edwin Peary (1856–1920), the arctic explorer who, with Matthew Henson, discovered the North Pole on April 6, 1909. When Peary returned to the United States he learned that Dr. Frederick Cook, who had accompanied him on a polar expedition in 1891–92, had claimed a prior discovery of the Pole for himself. A bitter controversy followed, but in 1911, Congress recognized Peary's claim, and he retired from the Navy with the rank of rear admiral. Further studies have confirmed Peary's claim, but there is still some uncertainty over whether Henson, an African American, may not have been the first person to stand at the Pole.

3. The Civil War. Laura was writing fifty-one years after the war's end, whereas we (in 1993) are reading her words seventy-seven years after they were written.

4. Missouri was established as a United States Territory in 1812, and became a state in 1821, around the time of the first wave of white settlement. The state's present boundaries were established in 1836, after Indian claims to what became Platte County were abandoned.

5. After the Civil War ended Missouri was plagued by outlaws like William Quantrill and his band of raiders, with whom Jesse James once rode.

6. The legend may refer to the gold-seeking conquistador, Hernando de Soto (1500-42), who discovered the Mississippi River and traveled up the Arkansas River at least as far as the Little Rock region.

7. A lean, wild-ranging hog, as distinct from the massive Duroc and Poland China breeds.

8. The celebrated judge of poultry described in the preceding article.

9. In Laura's time a suntan was considered lower class—a sign that one worked in the open air. In chapter 20 of *On the Banks of Plum Creek*, "School," Mary tells Laura to keep her sunbonnet on, or she'll be "brown as an Indian, and what will the town girls think of us?"

A Woman's Role

Good Times on the Farm

IT'S EASY TO HAVE FUN IF YOU PLAN FOR IT

Instead of being lonely, isolated, and bored, country women should get together!
Here Laura gives her women readers a few tips on socializing for survival.

*D*istances are long in the country, and although it is very pleasant to go and spend a day with a friend it takes a good while to see many people in that way. Women who have been rather isolated all summer need to be enlivened by seeing people, the more the better. There is something brightening to the wits and cheering to the spirits in congenial crowds that is found in nothing else.

Why not form a neighborhood club and combine the pleasure of going "a visiting" with the excitement of a little crowd and the joy of entertaining our friends all together when our turn comes? It is less trouble to entertain several at once than to entertain several times; besides there is a great saving of time, and as the club meets at first one house and then another, the neighborhood visiting is done with less work and worry, and more of pleasure than in any other way.

NEEDED BY COUNTRY WOMEN

It used to be that only the women in town would have the advantages of women's clubs, but now the woman in the country can be just as cultured a club woman as though she lived in town. The Neighborhood club can take up any line of work or study the members wish. Courses of reading can be obtained from the state university or the International Congress of Farm Women, and either organization will be glad to help with plans, advice and instruction. Bits of fancy work or sewing may be taken to the meetings and the latest stitch or short cut in plain sewing can be learned by all. Recipes may be exchanged, good stories told, songs sung and jokes enjoyed.

The serving of some dainty refreshments would add to the pleasure of the afternoon and keep the social graces in good practice. Women in the country as well as those in town need these occasions to show what charming hostesses and pleasant guests they can be. If the men folks want to go along, by all means let them do so. They might gather by themselves and discuss farm matters.[1] They might even organize and have a little farmers' club of their own, if they have not done so already; then they would be even more willing to hitch up and drive to the meeting place.

No Tiresome Meetings

There are so many ways to vary the meetings and programs they need never become tiresome or dull. Now and then the meeting may be held in the evening and an entertainment given by home talent. Sometimes the club might go in a body to a lecture or some amusement in town, or for a little excursion to the nearest city. A regular organization with the proper officers, a motto and membership badges will add to the interest, as will also being an auxiliary of some larger organization such as the International Congress of Farm Women.

Although the fall with its greater amount of leisure may be the best time to start a club of this kind, it need not be given up at the beginning of spring. The long, bright days of summer, when we all long to go picnicking and fishing, offer simply a different form of entertainment and social life and should be enjoyed to the full. Perhaps the meetings might best be farther apart while the rush of work is on, but a day off now and then will never be noticed in the work, and will do the workers a world of good.

The Best Books for Girls

A noted librarian has arranged a list of 10 books which have stood the wear and tear of the age of novels and are ever dear to the hearts of the maidens. He calls the set "Books That Are Popular With the Girls." They are:

Allen [James Lane]. *The Kentucky Cardinal*
A charming story of a Southern girl, a bachelor, and a bird.

Austen [Jane]. *Pride and Prejudice*
This concerns a man who was very proud and a girl who was very much prejudiced. It relates how they finally overcame these faults, to their mutual happiness.

Cooper [James Fenimore]. *The Last of the Mohicans*
Cooper's novels are always full of adventure. This is a tale of the last descendants of the Mohican tribe of Indians, which inhabited the Great Lakes region. The love element which runs through the story greatly adds to its interest.

Craik [Dinah Maria]. *John Halifax, Gentleman*
This novel has always been one of the girls' favorites. The story of a boy who struggles against poverty and hardship, and finally by means of his high principles and nobility of character, wins success and happiness—and the lady of his choice.

Montgomery [L.M.]. *Anne of Green Gables*
The story of a wholesome, bright, original girl who was adopted by an eccentric elderly couple, and who, by her cleverness and winsome ways, wins their hearts and overcomes their eccentricities.

Stevenson [Robert Louis]. *Treasure Island*
This story will interest boys and girls alike. It is a tale of sea pirates and is very thrilling and full of action and adventure.

Wallace [Lew]. *Ben Hur*
A story laid in the time of Christ. It is full of thrilling incidents and holds one's interest the whole way through.

Wiggin [Kate Douglas]. *Rebecca of Sunnybrook Farm*
Rebecca is one of seven brothers and sisters who live on Sunnybrook farm. She is taken to the city to live with her aunt, and while there and at school meets with many wonderful adventures.

Hughes. *The Old Nest*
A story that every girl ought to read. The old nest is the homestead from which a large family of children leave one by one to make nests of their own.

Norris [Kathleen]. *Mother*
The adventures of a girl who went to New York as private secretary to a prominent society woman.

A Homemaker of the Ozarks

MRS. DURNELL RECLAIMED A FARM, BUILT A HOUSE IN THE WILDERNESS AND LEARNED THE SECRET OF CONTENTMENT

Here Laura tells the success story of a woman after her own heart. Immediately following it is a letter from a less fortunate, and perhaps more typical, Ruralist reader.

Women have always been the home makers, but it is not usually expected of them that they should also be the home builders from the ground up. Nevertheless they sometimes are and their success in this double capacity shows what women can do when they try. Among the women who have done both is Mrs. C.A. Durnell of Mansfield, Mo. She has not only made a home but she has put a farm in condition to support it.

Mansfield is on the very crest of the Ozarks and the land is rough and hilly, covered with timber, where it has not been cleared. Although one of the most beautiful places in the world to live, with a soil repaying bountifully the care given to it, still it is no easy thing to make a farm out of a piece of the rough land. Imagine then the task for a woman, especially one with no previous experience of farming.

Mrs. Durnell was a city woman and for twenty years after her marriage, lived in St. Louis where her husband worked in the railroad terminal yards. Here she raised her three children until her eldest, a son, was through college and established in his profession.

None of the children were strong and about this time the second, a daughter, was taken sick with consumption, while the youngest, also a daughter, was threatened with the same disease. Hoping to restore their health, Mrs. Durnell brought them to the Ozarks, but too late to save the sick daughter.

As the other daughter showed signs of improvement, Mrs. Durnell decided to stay and the thought came to her to go on a little farm and make a home for her own and her husband's old age.

Sickness and the expense of living had used up the most of Mr. Durnell's wages as they went along and all they had to show for their twenty years of work was a house with a mortgage on it. Mrs. Durnell saw what so many do not realize until too late, that when Mr. Durnell became too old to hold his position any longer they would have no business of their own and quite likely no home either. A small farm, if she could get one running in good shape, would be a business of their own and a home where they could be independent and not fear the age limit.

Mr. Durnell stayed with his job in St. Louis, to be able to send what money he could spare to help in making the start.

They secured a farm of 23 acres a quarter of a mile from town. Ten acres was in an old wornout field that to use a local expression had been "corned to death;" 5 acres was in an old orchard, unkempt, neglected and grown up to wild blackberries. In the Ozark hills, neglected ground will grow up to wild blackberry briars, loaded with fruit in season. As the shiftless farmer said, "anyone can raise blackberries if he aint too durned lazy." Aside from this old orchard and wornout field, the place was covered with oak thicket where the land had been cleared and then allowed to go back. This second growth oak was about six feet high and as large around as a man's wrist. The fences were mostly down and such as were standing were the old worm, rail fence. The house was a log shack.

Mrs. Durnell and her daughter moved into the log house and went to work. They bought a cow to furnish them with milk and butter, but the cow would not stay inside the tumble-down fences, so repairing the fence was the first job. Some of it they built higher with their own hands and some they hired rebuilt, but there was only a little money to go on, so the work moved slowly. When the fences were in order and the cow kept at home they felt that a great deal had been gained.

The property in St. Louis was sold and after paying off the mortgage there was enough left to build a five room house, which Mr. Durnell planned and the construction of which she superintended. It was a happy day for them when they moved from the log cabin into the comfortable new house, although it stood in a thick patch of the oak thicket that made them feel terribly alone in the wilderness.

The crop the first year was 154 gallons of wild blackberries which grew in the orchard. There were no apples.

In the spring, Mrs. Durnell hired the 10 acre field broken; then she and her daughter planted it to corn. When the corn was large enough to be cultivated, a neighbor boy was hired to plow it and when he said the job was done she paid him for plowing the 10 acres. What was her surprise, some time later when walking across the field, to find that only ten rows on the outside of the field had been plowed and the rest was standing waist high in weeds. Since then she has personally overseen the work on the place.

Mrs. Durnell was learning by experience, also she was studying farming with the help of good farm papers and the state university and experiment stations. By the second spring she had learned better than to continue planting corn on the old field, so that spring she sowed it to oats and in the fall put it in wheat with a generous allowance of fertilizer. With the wheat she sowed 8 pounds of timothy seed to the acre and the next February 6 pounds of clover seed to the acre was sown over the field. When the wheat was cut the next summer there was a good stand of clover and timothy. The field was so rocky and brushy however that no one would cut the hay so the grass was wasted. This naturally suggested the next thing to be done, and the brush was sprouted out and the stones picked up, so that the grass could be cut; and the crop of hay secured.

A good many men have failed to raise alfalfa, in the hills, but Mrs. Durnell has succeeded. She says that care in preparing a good seedbed and plenty of fertilizer does the trick. The ground must be rich and the weeds must be worked out of it before alfalfa seed is sown, she says. One piece was sown in April and another was sown in September; both are a success.

The whole place is now cleared and seeded to grass, except in a little draw, where the timber is left to shade and protect the spring; and where the garden and berries grow.

Mrs. Durnell and her daughter cleared away some of the oak thicket and set out blackberries, raspberries, strawberries and grapes for home use. The wild blackberries have been cleaned out of the orchard, the apple trees trimmed, the ground cultivated and seeded to grass. Now there are plenty of apples and good grass for hay instead of wild blackberries and briars.

Gardening has been carefully studied; and the garden is always planned to raise the greatest variety and amount possible on the ground, and with the least labor. It is planted in long rows so that it can be plowed and leave very little to hand work. A furrow is plowed the length of the garden to plant the Irish potatoes in. These are dropped and lightly covered. This leaves them a little lower than the rest of the ground. As they are cultivated the dirt is thrown toward them and when they are cultivated for the last time they are hilled up, and the weeds have been kept down, all without any hand work. At the last cultivation kafir and milo are planed between the rows of potatoes and early garden stuff and there is plenty of time for it to mature and make fine large heads of grain for chicken feed.

Of all on her farm Mrs. Durnell is most interested in her flock of beautiful Rhode Island Reds. "I love them because they are so bright," she says, and they certainly seem to appreciate her kindness. Although they all look alike to a stranger, she knows every one by sight and calls them pet names as they feed from her hand. She knows which pullets lay the earliest and saves their eggs for hatching, for she has made a study of poultry as well as the other branches of farming, and knows that in this way she improves the laying qualities of the flock. "When starting my flock," says Mrs. Durnell, "I determined to have the best and I still get the best stock obtainable." She selects her breeders very carefully both for their early laying qualities and for their color and so has a flock of which any fancier might be proud as well as one that returns a good profit.

Everything is very carefully looked after on this little farm, nothing is wasted. The clearings from the poultry house are spread over the garden because there are no grass or weed seeds mixed with them to become a nuisance. The cleanings from the cow barn are spread over the meadows and if there is grass seed among them so much the better for the meadow.

Nor has the inside of the house been neglected because of the rush of work outside. Although this homemaker has learned to husband her strength and not do unnecessary things, still she has done the job thoroughly in the house also. Here are rare bits of old furniture brought from the old home, hand made, some of it, and hand carved. There is a fireplace made according to Mrs. Durnell's own plan, with a chimney that draws even though she had to stand by the mason as he was building it and insist that he build it as she directed. There are pictures and bits of china and there are books and papers everywhere, the daily paper and the latest novel mingling in pleasant companionship with farm papers and bulletins.

Mrs. Durnell says she never has a dull moment, because farming is so interesting. And one can understand the reason why, after being with her in the house and going around with her over the farm.

The whole place is carefully planned for beauty, as well as profit. The house is set on a rise of ground which adds much to its appearance and at the same time will allow of the whole place being overlooked as it can all be seen from the front porch and windows. Just south of the house is the old spring, where marching bands of soldiers used to drink in war time.

Not far away is the sink hole, a place where the rock shell of the hills is crushed in, making a cup shaped hollow in the ground, which gathers the water from the surrounding hills when it rains. This water pours down through a crack in the rock, sometimes as large around as a barrel in volume, to flow through the crevices and caverns of the hills, emerging later, when purified by its journey; and flowing away in springs and creeks to join the waters of the Gasconade.

Mrs. Durnell has made a beautiful home out of a rough, wild piece of land and a wornout field and she now feels that it is established on a permanent paying basis. The fruits and garden with the cow and chickens more than furnish the living. The farm is growing in value every day, without any more very strenuous efforts on her part; and the home that she and Mr. Durnell planned for their old age is theirs, because of her determination and great good sense.

It has taken a great deal of hard work to accomplish this desired end, but it has been done without any worry. Mrs. Durnell early decided that the burden was heavy enough without adding to it a load of worry and so she chose as a motto for her life and work: "Just do your best and leave the rest"—and this she has lived up to through it all.

Her only regret is that she did not come to the farm when her children were small, for she says: "There is no place like a farm for raising children, where they can have in such abundance the fresh air and sunshine, with pure living water, good wholesome food and a happy outdoor life."

The Best Place for a Woman

For Laura, the following reader's letter must have sounded a familiar, melancholy note. She and Almanzo had had their own share of suffering on a farm when they were first married, and she remembered those grim times vividly when she wrote an account of her early married life in *The First Four Years*; in particular, see her meditation near the beginning of chapter 1, "…a farm is such a hard place for a woman."

I am a farmer's wife in the Ozark country of southern Missouri, and I can tell you why I want my daughter to marry a city man. Nine tenths of farmers wives do work that I consider man's work, work such as hauling in feed, cutting up corn, providing fuel for winter fires and doing chores of various sorts. Woman, beautiful as she should be, as she was intended to be, cannot be her true self and look her best at work on a farm. I think a woman should be always clean, if clad in calico, with her hair arranged nicely, and her shoes well polished—ready to greet any neighbor or stranger who might call at her door. I love to see a clean woman in the yard tending her flock of chickens, or even hoeing in the garden, but I adore the womanly woman who has the house well kept. I do think that if a woman does her house work well, with her washing, ironing and mending, caring for her children, she has done her part. The country woman who has all the modern conveniences of her city sisters may find farm life a pleasure, but I for one have not been so blessed, and do not wish my daughters to experience what I have on the farm. We are poor and I help my husband. Don't think I write this through any disrespect for him. I love him, but I cannot love the farm.

—Mrs. A.B., Mountain View, Mo.

For Women's Rights

A *RURALIST* EDITORIAL

John F. Case, the Ruralist's *editor, was a sturdy advocate of women's rights, and here he spells out unambiguously why that is.*

Missouri has been made a great agricultural state because of the self-sacrificing effort of its womankind. We hear much about the man who produced the record yield of grain, or the prize winning car of cattle, but little about his partner who worked longer hours during the hot summer months and made it possible for him to give his entire attention to the business on hand. The heroes of a naval battle are the keen sighted men who handle the guns, but none the less heroic and entitled to credit are the grimy stokers in the bowels of the ship. Each does his allotted part and does it well. It has been said that "an army marches upon its stomach," and it is none the less true that an army toiling in the field from sun to sun must be well fed if the fight against all the adverse elements of nature is to be won. Mother, in charge of the kitchen brigade, should share equal rank with father, head of the warriors against weeds.

What does mother get for being the commanding officer of the food forces? Board and clothes usually and the satisfaction that comes from knowing that you have done your best. Father sells the dollar wheat that buys another "40" although there was already ample land for all the family needs. The "hog money" goes for labor saving machinery, all very necessary, but no more necessary than kitchen conveniences that could be installed for half the sum and would mean added efficiency as well as comfort. Certainly it is true that Missouri has farm homes well equipped with labor saving devices, homes with running water, lights and heating plants, but the number is so lamentably small even where the owners are worth thousands of dollars that it wouldn't be worth publishing. What we need more than suffrage in Missouri is woman's rights, an equal share of the money earned. We should like to hear of some real partnerships on Missouri farms. Perhaps we are unduly pessimistic but it doesn't seem to us that Missouri farm women are getting their rightful share of the good things of life.

—John F. Case, editor, Missouri *Ruralist*

Folk are "Just Folks"

WHY SHOULDN'T TOWN AND COUNTRY WOMEN
WORK AND PLAY TOGETHER?

Laura was not just a notable figure in farm matters, she was also a leader in Wright County's intellectual life, and an untiring advocate of self-improvement by reading and discussion. She was, after all, a pioneer woman, and pioneer women were always, though rarely acknowledged as such, the principle guardians of civilization on the frontier. Here she describes a club, principally for women, that she help to found in Wright County to encourage reading and intellectual pursuits.

The Little House books are full of descriptions of the pleasure the Ingalls family found in reading. Among the books Laura mentions in her novels are the poems of Tennyson (a Christmas gift), the Waverly novels by Sir Walter Scott, Prescott's *Conquest of Mexico* and *Conquest of Peru*, a work called *Ancient and Medieval History*, and Fenimore Cooper's *The Leatherstocking Tales*. There was also Pa's much loved big, green *Wonders of the Animal World* (which he reads aloud from in *The Long Winter*, while the children pretend that "the wind is lions roaring").

The family also read eagerly awaited periodicals, *Youth's Companion*, *Godey's Lady's Book*, *Pioneer News*, *Advance*, *Inter-Ocean*, and the *New York Ledger*, from which, in chapter 22 of *By the Shores of Silver Lake*, Laura reads aloud "...a wonderful story, about dwarfs and caves where robbers lived and a beautiful lady who was lost in the caves."

"The Athenians," is a woman's club just lately organized in Hartville, for purposes of study and self-improvement. Hartville[2] was already well supplied with social organizations. There was an embroidery club also a whist club and the usual church aid societies and secret orders which count for so much in country towns. Still there were a few busy women who felt something was lacking. They could not be satisfied altogether with social affairs. They wanted to cultivate their minds and increase their knowledge, so they organized the little study club and have laid out a year's course of study.

The membership of the club is limited to twenty. If one of the twenty drops out then some one may be elected to take the vacant place. Two negative ballots exclude anyone from membership. There are no dues. "The Athenians" is, I think, a little unique for a town club, as the membership is open to town and country women alike and there are several country members. Well, why not? "The Colonel's lady and Judy O'Grady are sisters under the skin." (Mind I have not said whether Judy O'Grady is a town or country woman. She is just as likely, if not a little more likely, to be found in one place as the other).

Surely the most vital subjects in which women are interested are the same in town and country, while the treasures of literature and the accumulated knowledge of the world are for all alike. Then why not study them together and learn to know each other better? Getting acquainted with folks makes things pleasanter all around. How can we like people if we do not know them? It does us good to be with people whose occupation and surroundings are different from ours. If their opinions differ from ours, it will broaden our minds to get their point of view and we will likely find that they are right in part at least, while it may be that a mutual understanding will lead to a modification of both opinions.

While busily at work one afternoon I heard the purr of a motor and going to the door to investigate, I was met by the smiling faces of Mr. and Mrs. Frink and Mr. and Mrs. Curtis of Hartville. Mrs. Curtis and Mrs. Frink have taken an active part in organizing "The Athenians" and they had come over to tell me of my election to membership in that club. What should be done when there is unexpected company and one is totally unprepared and besides must be at once hostess, cook and maid? The situation is always easily handled in a story. The lovely hostess can perform all kinds of conjuring tricks with a cold bone and a bit of left over vegetable, producing a delicious repast with no trouble whatever and never a smut on her beautiful gown. In real life it sometimes is different, and during the first of that pleasant afternoon my thoughts would stray to the cook's duties. When the time came, however, it was very simple. While I made some biscuit, Mrs. Frink fried some home cured ham and fresh eggs, Mrs. Curtis set the table. The Man Of The Place opened a jar of preserves and we all had a jolly, country supper together before the Hartville people started on the drive home. It is such a pleasure to have many friends and to have them dropping in at unexpected times that I have decided when it lies between friendships and feasting and something must be crowded out the feasting may go every time.

At a recent meeting of "The Athenians" some very interesting papers, prepared by the members were read. Quoting from the paper read by Mrs. George Hunter: "The first societies of women were religious and charitable. These were followed by patriotic societies and organizations of other kinds. At present there exists in the United States a great number of clubs for women which may be considered as falling under the general heads—educational, social and practical. The clubs which may be classified as practical include charitable organizations, societies for civic improvement or for the furthering of schools, libraries, and such organizations as have for their object the securing, by legislation, of improved conditions for working women and children. In 1890 the General Federation of Women's Clubs was formed. There were in the United States at the last enumeration more than 200,000 women belonging to clubs." Get the number? Two hundred thousand! Quite a little army this.

A very interesting paper and one that causes serious thought was that prepared by Mrs. Howe Steel on "The Vocation of Woman." "Woman," says Mrs. Steel, "has found out that with education and freedom, pursuits of all kinds are open to her and by following these pursuits she can preserve her personal liberty, avoid the grave responsibilities, the almost inevitable sorrows and anxieties which belong to family life. She can choose her friends and change them. She can travel and gratify her tastes and satisfy her personal ambitions. The result is that she frequently is failing to discharge satisfactorily some of the most imperative demands the nation makes upon her. I think it was Longfellow who said: 'Homekeeping hearts are happiest.' Dr. Gilbert said, 'Thru women alone can our faintest dreams become a reality. Woman is the creator of the future souls unborn. Tho she may be cramped, enslaved and hindered, tho she may never be able to speak her ideal, or touch the work she longs to accomplish, yet in the prayer of her soul is the prophecy of her destiny.'

> Here's to woman the source of all our bliss,
> There's a foretaste of Heaven in her kiss.
> From the queen upon her throne to the maiden in her dairy,
> They are all alike in this.

In "Soldiers of the Soil," a story by Rose Wilder Lane [Laura's daughter], a real country woman says: "It is my opinion there are lots more happy homes in the country than there are in the city. If everybody lived in the country you wouldn't hear all this talk about divorce." I wonder how true that is and if true, or if not true, what are the reasons for it? I suppose there are statistics on the subject. There are on most things, but you know "there are three kinds of lies— lies, d— lies and statistics," so why bother about them? The reasons given by the women quoted were that while the women in the country worked, to help out the family income, her work was at home, while if the woman in the city worked she must leave her home to do so; that, working together, man and wife were drawn together, while working apart they drifted apart.

There may be fewer divorces in the country without it necessarily following that there are more happy homes. It seems to me that the deadly monotony of working with, and playing with, the same person in the same place for days and weeks and months and years would be more apt to drive a person to divorce or suicide than if they were separated during the working day and could meet when it was over with different experiences to speak about and to add variety to their companionship. To be sure, in the city a woman can live in one apartment as well as another so long as her pay envelope comes to hand regularly, while in the country when a woman leaves her home she leaves her job too. Perhaps this has more effect in lessening divorce in the country than the happy home idea. We carry our own environment with us to a certain extent and are quite likely to stand or fall by the same principles wherever we may live.

Each in his Own Place

I know a farm woman who is wearing overalls this spring at her outdoor work. "They wear overalls in the munitions factories,"[3] she says. "Isn't the raising of food to preserve life as important as the making of shells to take it? Why should I be hampered in my work and tormented by skirts flapping around my ankles when I am out in the field?"

Why indeed! When every bit of one's time and strength can be put to such good use in work that is so very necessary to the world, it seems foolish to spend any of it uselessly. The simpler and more suitably we can dress the better. This year of our Lord 1917 is no time for giving much attention to frills and when we remember the tight skirts of recent date, we surely cannot accuse overalls of being immodest. As the Man of the Place said to me, "Just hunt up a couple of your old tight skirts and sew them together, then you'll have a pair of overalls."

We all feel that we would like to do something to help our country in these perilous times, however much we may regret the necessity. We may do this; may do our share of the work and bear our share of the burden of the world without leaving our homes or exposing ourselves to new and fearful dangers. Not that country women would hesitate to take these risks if it were necessary, but it is natural to be glad that we may help as much or more in our accustomed ways. Women in the towns and cities can be spared to work in the factories, to make munitions, to join the navy or to go as nurses with the Red Cross, but what would happen to the world if the farm women should desert their present posts?

Our work is not spectacular and in doing it faithfully we shall win no war medals or decorations, but it is absolutely indispensable. We may feed the field hands, care for the poultry and work in the garden with the full assurance that we are doing as much for our country as any other person. Here in the Hills we have helped plant the potatoes and corn, we help with the milking and feed the calves and hogs and we will be found on the line just behind the trenches, "fighting for Uncle Sam," as I heard one woman say, and every extra dozen eggs, pound of meat or bushel of vegetables we raise will help beat back the enemy, hunger.

Some women were talking over an entertainment that had been planned for the crowd. They seemed to be taking only a half-hearted interest in the subject and finally one of them exclaimed: "I can't feel right about doing this! It does not seem to me that this is a time to be feasting and frolicking. I do not think we ought to eat an unnecessary mouthful and sometimes I feel like choking on the food I do eat when I think of the people in the world who are hungry and starving."

I fully agreed with her. When there seems not enough food to go around, we ought to be as careful and economical with it as possible. If it is true, as we are told, that most of us have the bad habit of overeating, now is a good time to break that habit.

I am sure that we farm women will not be found second to those of any other occupation in willingness to bear our part in effort or in self denial, and if, as experts say, "armies travel on their stomachs," we are doing our best to enable the soldiers of the United States to go as far as those of any other nation.

Without Representation

In answer to the call sent out by the State College of Agriculture, the park in Mansfield was filled with a crowd of farm folks and town folks to listen to the address of the man from the college who was organizing farmers' clubs thru the county. As I looked around at the people, I thought what a representative gathering it was. Judging from the appearance of the crowd, the women were as much interested in the subject of food production as a means of national defense as the men were, for fully as many women as men were present and they were seemingly as eager to learn from the speaker anything that farmers could do to increase the food supply. A farmers' club was formed after the address but the women took no part in the organization nor were they included in any way. As arrangements were being made for a meeting of the club, some one near the speaker said, "The women must come too," but it was only after a broad and audible hint from a woman that this remark was made and it was so plainly because of this hint, instead of from a desire for the womens' presence and co-operation, that it made no impression.

At the first meeting of the club, the following week, there were only two women present. Quite likely it was the women's own fault and if they had taken part as a matter of course it would have been accepted as such, but it seems rather hard to do this unless we are shown the courtesy of being mentioned. We will get over this feeling in time no doubt and take the place we should, for a farmer may be either a man or a woman and farmers' clubs are intended for both.

Everyone knows that women raise the poultry and Missouri receipts from poultry products are more than from cattle, horses and mules combined. If farm women refused to help in the work of the farm how much difference do you suppose it would make in the output of dairy products?

What would happen to the "increase of production," if the women did not cook for the harvest hands, to say nothing of taking care of the hired help for the remainder of the year?

A man in authority at Washington urges farm women to increase their power of production and all along down the line, agricultural colleges, farmers' club organizers, domestic science lecturers and farm papers join in the urge.

"Raise more garden truck; increase the egg production; caponize the cockerels and keep them until they will yield more meat to the fowl when killed; feed the calves and let them grow up instead of selling them for veal." (Who feeds the calves?) "Can; pickle; preserve and dry fruits and vegetables; let nothing go to waste from the garden or orchard."

As one farm paper says, "The women and children can do it!" "Eliminate all waste from the kitchen! It is conceded that it will take more time and work to do all this but it is patriotic duty and will increase farm profits." Why shouldn't farm women's work be recognized by state authorities and others in other ways than urging her to more and yet more work when her working day is already somewhere from 14 to 16 hours long?

There is a woman's commission of the Council of National Defense and under this commission committees are being organized in every state for the purpose of co-operating with the National Woman's Trade Union league of America. The league is fighting to protect the women and children who are working in factories and in the cities. It asks that the American people demand the 8-hour day, the living wage and one day of rest in seven.

But mark this! These things are for women and children working in the cities. They are not intended to extend to the women and children on farms. There is not as yet, so far as I know, any committee to co-operate with the farm women in obtaining for them either an 8-hour day or a living profit and if they are denied an active part in the farmers' clubs they are the only class of workers who are absolutely without representation.

Did the farmers' club organized in your neighborhood recognize the women and if so in what way? We would all be interested to know. Write to me and tell me about it!

And a Woman Did It

THE WILSON STOCK FARM IS ONE OF MISSOURI'S BEST

This article tells the story of another rural heroine. It is calculated to inspire and raise the spirits of Laura's readers, and is followed, for the younger set, by a letter from a gutsy thirteen-year-old.

Down in the Ozarks, in Wright county, Missouri, is a 1000-acre farm where the purebred Shorthorn cattle and registered Poland China hogs roam over blue grass and clover pastures in the sunny days of summer time and in winter feast on bright alfalfa hay and succulent silage. These upper class animals come of aristocratic lineage and are cared for royally and this stock farm is managed by a woman and has been brought up from a rundown "hog and hominy" farm to its present state of efficiency by her knowledge, hard work and good business judgment.

A part of the present Wilson farm owned by Dr. and Mrs. Wilson, late of St. Louis, was bought by them 13 years ago. While on a visit to relatives in Wright county, Dr. Wilson became so enamored of the Ozarks as a place to make a home that he tried to by a small farm near the one he now owns, but failed to obtain it and went back to St. Louis disappointed. Some time later a brother-in-law wrote him that a small place, adjoining the one he had wished to purchase, could be bought at a reasonable figure and that he would take charge and manage it for them.

So the farm was bought and stocked and the brother-in-law took charge but that was as far as he kept his agreement. He did not stay to manage. Becoming possessed of the idea that he could do better for himself farther west, he left the Wilson farm at a moment's notice.

The farm was well stocked with common stock and a good deal of money had been spent for them and for farming tools as well as for the farm itself. Dr.

Wilson could not leave his practice in the city without too great a sacrifice, neither could he take it with him, so it became necessary that Mrs. Wilson should save the investment and come to the rescue of the home that was to be. Both of these things she has done and more. Not only has she saved what was then put into the place but she has more than trebled the original investment. Other tracts of land have been added to the first small place until there is now, to be exact, 997 acres in the Wilson farm. This land was purchased for $10 and $12 an acre and is now easily worth from $30 to $50 and acre.

"All I know about farming," said Mrs. Wilson, "I have learned since we bought Fern Cliff. This is the real name of the farm. The neighbors began calling it the Wilson farm and it has gone by that name, but I always call it Fern Cliff to myself." The name was chosen because of a very beautiful spot on the farm where the face of a sheer cliff is nearly covered with lovely drooping ferns.

"I was born on the farm," continued Mrs. Wilson, "and from the age of 9 until I was 14 I lived with my grandparents on their place in the country, but I always hated it and thought the worst calamity that could befall me would be to marry a farmer and live on a farm. This thought was a real nightmare to me and I always said it was one thing I would never do, but the old saying has proved true that 'what you say you will not do, that you have to do.'"

Mrs. Wilson has learned the business of farming and stock breeding from books and farm papers, attending farmers' meetings, talking with other farmers and breeders and from practical experience. The Wilson farm was the first in this part of the Ozarks to have a field of alfalfa. Having read about alfalfa, it was decided to try it and 4 acres were sown. It made a good catch and so 20 acres more were seeded. This also was a success. Mrs. Wilson has been generous and the soil from this field has gone to many other farms to inoculate the soil for growing alfalfa. The spirit of the farming operations on the Wilson farm is shown in Mrs. Wilson's answer to a question. "No," she said, "I did not send any soil away to be analyzed. I read about alfalfa and I just tried it."

There are 400 acres in cultivation on the Wilson farm. The rest is pasture and woodland. Corn, wheat, oats and hay are raised on the place, in addition to the alfalfa.

"After taking charge," said Mrs. Wilson, "I soon learned to love the stock, especially the cattle which at that time were grades. I decided that it took no longer to raise and care for purebreds than it did grades and so we looked around for something better. I had no knowledge of stock except horses. Grandfather was from Kentucky and knew and kept good horses and he always said that I could point my finger at the best one every time, but I have learned about cattle since I began farming."

Mrs. Wilson became quite enthusiastic when asked why they chose the Shorthorn Durham cattle. After enumerating their many good qualities she summed it up thus: "The Shorthorns have all other breeds beaten when it comes to making money for their owners. Besides they are aristocrats and we think them the most beautiful of any." Trust a woman to think of that last reason.

The animals on the Wilson farm are certainly aristocrats. The first Shorthorn owned on the place was a son of Lavender Viscount many times champion and grand champion at the American Royal Stock show of Kansas City and the International of Chicago. Next came Champion Monarch from Purdy Brothers' herd, Harris, Missouri, and now the head of the herd is Violet Chief out of the herd of N.H. Gentry, of Sedalia, Missouri. Good females have been bought from time to time and there is now on the Wilson farm a herd of 100 head of purebred Shorthorns as fine as one would care to see.

Nothing seems to have been overlooked, that makes for success on this farm owned and operated by these city people who have "gone back to the land." Beside the registered Shorthorn cattle and Poland China hogs there is on the place a flock of purebred Bronze turkeys. From the flock of 34 raised four years ago, the number has increased to 100 and during these four years they have brought in, in cash, $781.92.

"I farmed at first because it was necessary," says Mrs. Wilson. "Now I farm because I like it. Dr. Wilson, from the first, has been more in love with the farm than I have been. He knows nothing about the stock or farming because he has been tied to his practice in the city, but now he has given it up and come home to the farm he can learn as I did." Dr. Wilson fully intends to do so, but already his professional services are being called for and he may not be allowed time.

This building of a farm business literally "from the ground up" has been no light task. Mrs. Wilson says that most of the time she is "too busy to think twice in the same place." She is very modest about what she has accomplished but the beautiful Wilson farm with its rich bottom fields and rolling pasture lands, with its silos and barns and stacks of alfalfa and above all the fine stock at home on the place speak for her.

This Girl Can Farm

FROM "THEY ARE HELPING UNCLE SAM: BY THE BOYS AND GIRLS"

I drilled 13 acres of corn once and part of it twice and replanted and hoed most of it. Besides this I made a garden of my own consisting of onions, tomatoes, cabbages, radishes, lettuce and beets. I milk two cows twice a day, take them to and from the pasture, and pump water for the stock. I help my father water and take care of the horses. We have two little colts that I like to play with.

I put in all my idle moments peeling apples to can and dry and helping mother in the kitchen. My mother gave me some eggs and the use of a hen, and I now have 20 large fries. I also have 14 young guineas almost large enough to fry. I am 13 years old. I hope we can win the war.

—Agnes Spencer, Gentry, Mo.

What the War Means to Women

World War I, during which many women proved that they could "do a man's work," clinched the success of the movement for women's rights. (The 19th Amendment, granting nationwide suffrage to women, was ratified by Congress on August 26, 1920.) In this and the next article, Laura's belief in the natural justice of equality between men and women becomes passionate when she considers the atrocities (some of them, we now know, only the fictions of propaganda) committed by men against women in the Great War. In "New Day for Women," she foresees that things will change for the better.

"This is a woman's war and the women will see to it that before the war is ended the world shall be made safe for women." This sentiment was expressed by a woman in my hearing soon after the declaration of war by the United States.

Every war is more or less a woman's war, God knows, but is this in an especial way a woman's war? Never before in the history of the world has war been deliberately made upon the womanhood of the world and motherhood, woman's crown and glory, been made her scourge and shame. The tortures by savages, tales of which used to make our blood run cold did not equal in horror and cruelty what has been inflicted upon educated, refined women and ignorant peasant women alike.

Stripped naked and driven along the roads out of their own country a sport for drunken soldiery. Thrown by hundreds into the rivers when the crowds of soldiers had tired of them—this was part of the war in Armenia.

Death by thousands, after nameless horrors and suffering, along the roads of Poland!

Driven over the snow covered mountains of Servia [Serbia]; dying of hunger and exhaustion and wounds, a fate preferred to falling into the hands of the invaders—this was the fate of the women of Servia.

Tortured and defiled, mutilated and murdered in Belgium and northern France! The mind revolts and the soul sickens at even trying to contemplate the things that women have been made to suffer by Germany's invading armies.

There has been a planned, deliberate attempt, by the enemy, to destroy the other nations of the world. To destroy a nation, its women and children must be exterminated and so a part of this incredible plot has been to so mutilate and destroy the women of those nations that they will bear no more children to perpetuate their race.

All over the world women are bravely taking their part in the conflict and doing what they can to defend those things they hold most sacred, their homes, their children and their honor. In all the allied countries women are filling places of responsibility and danger, doing hard, unpleasant work to help in the struggle to "make the world safe for women."

Women are showing their fearlessness on all the battle fronts. In Russia when the soldiers refused to fight, the women formed the famous "Battalion of Death" and met the enemy on the first line. They held their section of the line, too, when on every side the soldiers retreated in disorder and tho every woman in the battalion was killed or wounded. Later, with their ranks refilled, this battalion of women took part in the fighting at Petrograd, defending their position dauntlessly, seemingly without fear of death.

The women in the Red Cross units on the western front hesitate at nothing they find to do to help the allied cause. They were the last to leave the abandoned towns before the Germans entered and they helped the refugees to escape, picked up and removed scores of wounded, driving their own trucks and motor cars, established temporary kitchens near the front to feed the soldiers who had not eaten for hours and, when the emergency arose, took charge of the military traffic and directed the columns of guns, cavalry, supply wagons and troops and prevented a traffic jam.

The women of the American Red Cross are winning honor on the western battle front. They act as cooks or chauffeurs, traffic policemen, stretcher bearers or grave diggers as the occasion arises.

Women in sheltered America have perhaps been slow to realize what the war means to them but they are beginning to understand. Among them, as among the men, are some pessimists and whiners, also some cowards and slackers, but they are few.

When the British retreated on the west, the first of April, a man remarked,

"They're licking the stuffing out of us, licking us every day," and a woman answered, "What does one retreat amount to? A man isn't whipped in a fight even if he is knocked down, if he just gets up and comes again."

I like the spirit of the man whom I heard say, "We can't be whipped! We won't be whipped! We'll fight for 60 years if we must, but we'll never give up!"

A widow whose son volunteered and is now in France, said she was so proud of him that she had no time to be sorry; that she could not understand how any young man could stay at home.

Another woman, speaking of her son who had volunteered, said she was proud of him and that he would have been ashamed to look his sister in the face if he had not gone to help protect her from the fate of the girls of Belgium and France.

The congregation at the church was remarkable on Easter Sunday for the absence of new hats and the large number of Liberty Bond pins and Red Cross buttons. One woman who has always taken great pride in her appearance said to me: "I can't get a new hat this summer. I'm paying for my Liberty Bond and helping with the Red Cross and someway new hats don't seem to matter."

The little town of Mansfield and immediate vicinity, oversubscribed its quota in the Third Liberty Loan.

A New Day for Women

How long has it been since you saw an old maid? Oh, of course, one sees unmarried women every day, but it has been a good many years since I have seen a real "old maid" or "maiden lady." Even the terms sound strange and lead one back and back into memories. There were old maids when I was a girl. Later some of the older girls protested against being called old maids and insisted upon being called "bachelor girls." There was some controversy over whether women should be given such a title, I remember, but not having any special interest in the subject, I lost sight of it and awakened later to the fact that both old maids and bachelor girls had disappeared, how or when I do not know. In their place are simply women, young women, older women, (never old women), married and unmarried women, divorced women and widows, with the descriptive adjective in the background, but nowhere in the world, I think, are there any old maids.

As one considers the subject, it becomes plain that this one fact contains the whole story and explanation of the change in the world of women, the broadening and enriching of their lives. In the days when old maids flourished, the one important fact in a woman's life was whether or not she were married and as soon as a girl child reached maturity she was placed in one of two classes and labeled accordingly. She was either Mrs.——or else an old maid.

THE WORLD IS OPEN TO US

As women became more interested in other things; as the world opened up to them its storehouse of activities and absorbing interests; when the fact that a woman was a doctor, a lawyer, a farmer or what not; when her work in and for the world became of more importance than her private life, the fact of whether or not she were married did not receive the emphasis that it formerly did. To be sure, everyone knows that a woman's most important work is still her children, but other interests enter so largely into her life today that she is not classified solely on the one count. Altho still a vital part of a woman's life, marriage is not now the end and aim of her existence. There are in the world, many, many other ambitions and occupations to take up her attention.

Women are successful lumber dealers, livestock breeders, caterers, curators, bacteriologists, pageant managers, cable code experts and besides have entered nearly every ordinary profession. They have learned and are learning the most advanced methods of farming and scientific dairy management while it has become no uncommon thing for a woman to manage an ordinary farm. The exigencies of the war have thrust women into many new occupations that otherwise they might not have undertaken for many years if ever. Thousands of them have become expert munition makers and, while we all hope there will be no need for that trade when the present war is ended, still there will be use for the trained technical skill which these women workers have acquired.

Women are running trains, they are doing the work in factories, they are clerks, jurors, representatives in congress and farm help. By the time the war is over most of the economic and industrial systems of the world will be in the hands of the women. Quite likely, too, they will have, thru the ballot, the control of the political governments of the world.

If by an inconceivable turn of fate, Germany should conquer in the struggle now going on, women will be held in control by the military power and without doubt will be again restricted to the home and children, according to the rule laid down by Emperor Wilhelm defining their sphere of activity, but this we will not permit to be possible.

When the democratic nations are victorious and the world is ruled by the ballot instead of cannon, there is scarcely a doubt but what women will be included the universal suffrage. Already the franchise has been given to 6 million women in England. A suffrage amendment to the constitution of the United States missed being brought before congress by only a few votes and there is no doubt but that the women of the United States will soon have the ballot.

In Russia when the Revolution occurred, the women took the franchise with the men as a matter of course and without question. In France the old idea that women should rule thru their influence over men is still alive but growing feeble. More and more women and men are coming to stand together on terms of frankness and equality.

WOMEN SHALL RULE

Italy is far behind the other nations in the emancipation of its women, still the women of Italy have a great influence. It was the use of German propaganda among the Italian peasant women that weakened Italy and caused the late reverses there.[4]

We all realize, with aching hearts, that there is a great slaughter of men on the battle fronts and with the sexes about equal over the world before the war, what will be the result when millions of men are killed? When at last the "Beast of Berlin" is safely caged and the soldiers of freedom return home to settle quietly down into civil life once more, the women are going to be largely in the majority over the world. With the ballot in their hands, they are going to be the rulers of a democratic world.

There is a great deal of speculation about the conditions that will prevail after the war. Nearly all writers and thinkers are looking for a new order, a sort of social and industrial revolution and they all expect it to come thru the returned soldiers. No one, so far as I have found, is giving a thought to the fact that in a free democratic world, the power will be in the hands of the women who have stayed quietly at home working, sorrowing and thinking.

Will we be wise and true and strong enough to use this power for the best, or will we be deceived thru our ignorance or driven on the wrong way by storms of emotion or enthusiasm? We have been privileged to look on and criticize the way the world has been run. "A man-made world" we have called it now and then, implying that women would have done so much better in managing its affairs. The signs indicate that we are going to have a chance to remake it nearer to the heart's desire. I wish I might be sure that we would be equal to our opportunity.

I suggested this idea of the coming powers of women, to a liberal-minded man, a man who is strongly in favor of woman suffrage and he replied: "The women are no more ready for such a responsibility than the people of Russia were; they are ignorant along the lines of government and too uncontrolled in their emotions."

I wonder if he is right! The majority vote in a Democratic league of nations will be a great power to hold in inexperienced hands; a great responsibility to rest upon the women of the world.

In Reply to Mrs. Wilder

A female opponent of woman's suffrage gives Laura a stern rebuff, in terms that are still familiar.

I read the "New Day for Women" in the Woman's Special number of the Missouri *Ruralist*, and being a very old-fashioned woman I should like to express my views. I don't think it ever was intended for women to rule. We are not built that way. If that day ever comes we will have to do away with our dear old Bible. God is Ruler of the universe and He made man in His image, therefore men should rule. We are not capable of running our own affairs, much less ruling the men.

It is perfectly right for women to work but I am very sorry to think that they may have to don man's apparel and make such a hub-bub about what they do. Why can't we do as our good old great grandmothers did in the days gone by? There never was a time when some women did not do the work of men but they have been modest about it. Where is our modesty today? Those who wear enough clothing worth mentioning want it to be as mannish as possible. And they even ride like men. Our foreparents would blush if they could see the women of today. It will be a sad day if the women rule. It is at home that we should rule, and our rulership should be one of love and kindness. So far as voting is concerned I never would vote if I had the chance.

Now that our finest specimens of manhood are being taken away I think it very unjust to seem elevated over the idea of ruling what is left. I might ask, for what are they fighting? We should encourage and help them all that we can but one earnest prayer is worth more than a dozen suffragette.[5]

We farm women have our place and our work and so have the women of the cities. May God help us to fill our place in life and in service as He intended us to do.

—Mrs. F.P.M

Notes for "A Woman's Role"

1. Clear evidence that women are those who foster culture: women will get reading lists from the State University—men will discuss farm matters.

2. The county seat of Wright County, 12 miles north of Laura's home town, Mansfield.

3. The United States had broken off diplomatic relations with Germany in February of 1917, and had entered World War I on the side of the Allies on April 6.

4. The subject of Laura's singular diagnosis may be Italy's disastrous defeat by the Austrians at the battle of Caporetto in late 1917. On November 3, 1918, the Italians defeated the Austrians at the battle of Vittorio Veneto, and thus forced the Austrian surrender.

5. Mrs. F. P. M. here uses the derogatory form of "suffragist "